How to Start a Podcast

An Essential Guide to Profitable Podcasting for Beginners

Table of Contents

Introduction
Chapter 1: The Podcasting World Explained
Chapter 2: Pinpointing Your Niche and Audience
Chapter 3: Branding and Planning Your Content
Chapter 4: Podcasting Equipment for All Budgets
Chapter 5: Recording Your First Podcast
Chapter 6: Editing and Post-Production
Chapter 7: The Writing Stuff: Show Notes and Transcripts
Chapter 8: Where and How to Upload Your Podcast
Chapter 9: Podcasting for Profit: 10 Ways to Monetize Your Podcast
Chapter 10: Marketing Your Podcast
Chapter 11: Guest Interviewing Skills
Conclusion

Introduction

Firstly, we need to define what exactly a podcast is. A podcast is a regular Internet show, which can be an interview, commentary, monologue, or a series of vignettes. The content for a podcast is typically audio but can include text and still images, too. This comprehensive guide to podcasting will help you design, plan, execute, and promote your podcast.

The first chapter explains the podcasting world and how you can get started to create your podcast. This chapter has all the information you need if you are new to publishing or are looking for different ways to use your writing skills.

The second chapter covers what you need to know about finding your niche and audience, understanding what kind of content they want, spotting where gaps in the market lie, and how to put together a good podcasting strategy.

The third chapter focuses on your brand and planning your content and the structure of a typical podcast show without it sounding formulaic or boring!

The fourth chapter then looks at different equipment options for recording podcasts.

The fifth chapter focuses on recording your first podcast, including the equipment, software, and potential challenges you may face. It also looks at other technologies, such as Anchor and GarageBand.

The sixth chapter is all about editing a podcast where you look at what types of edits can be done to improve a show and how to handle silence optimally.

The seventh chapter is all about the written material that goes along with a podcast. This includes show notes and transcripts, each of which has pros and cons, depending on your audience's needs.

The eighth chapter looks at how you go about uploading your podcast to different platforms so it can be downloaded onto people's devices. Once they have downloaded the podcast episode, they can listen to it offline without an Internet connection.

The ninth chapter focuses on how you can take your podcast to the next level by making money from it in various ways. This chapter dispels some of the myths surrounding how much money a podcaster can make from their podcast. You will also look at monetization for different business models and whether you should podcast for free or charge money in return.

The tenth chapter focuses on promoting your podcast to get more listeners. It also looks at some common mistakes that podcasters make when they are just starting out and offers advice on avoiding them.

Finally, the last chapter is all about interviewing guests on your podcast and how you can get the best results from a guest interview. This chapter advises on simple techniques such as "pitching" your guest, what to do if they refuse to answer questions, and how to ask the right questions during an interview so that you get the content you need.

The chapters are not too long, which means that you can work your way through them quickly. You can then start podcasting straight away. If you have been thinking about starting a podcast, this guide will help you do so quickly and easily.

Chapter 1: The Podcasting World Explained

The podcasting world is a rather mysterious one for those who have not studied or researched it. Unlike video and written content, podcast production and distribution processes are neither popular nor easily understandable. Of course, this is not to say that podcasts are a complex medium. In fact, they are quite the opposite. However, starting a podcast requires a good deal of mental effort—at least if you want to create a good podcast. That is why the best way to start you on this journey is by giving you the lowdown on the podcasting world and podcasts as a medium before looking at the stages of production and distribution in depth.

What Is Podcasting?

Technically speaking, podcasts are a series of audio, spoken-word episodes that can be streamed or downloaded and listened to at one's leisure.

Four Elements That Define Podcasts

1. **Audio**

Podcasts are an audio-centric medium. However, this does not mean they lack a visual component by way of video. Being an audio-based medium means that podcasts have their unique way of writing and structuring. Just like a radio show is not a movie that lacks video, podcasts are not lacking anything. They are simply their own medium.

2. **Host/Actors/Characters**

While podcasts often feature different interviewees, there needs to be an anchor host or a duo whose job is to engage listeners. A host creates the brand, vibe, and atmosphere that attracts the listener. They also act as the main character. They should have an attractive personality that shows through their manner of speech, and through that, they connect with their audience. On a basic level, the consistency of having one host is comforting for listeners. On a higher emotional level, the host-listener connection is one factor that keeps audiences coming back for more.

Of course, when it comes to fiction narrative story podcasts, the voice actors/characters/stories are responsible for creating this emotional connection.

3. **Consistency**

As with TV series, podcasts come in all types of formats, and they have all kinds of themes. The key is to select a format and a theme and then stick to them. You could also opt for an anthology podcast that presents changing stories/themes. Otherwise, it is not a podcast as much as it's a collection of recordings. To show how true this is, let us look at some case studies.

The 2021 hit comedy true-crime podcast, "My Favorite Murder," by comedians Karen Kilgariff and Georgia Hardstark, covers different murders in every episode. So, while there is a different theme and topic covered within each episode, there's also a general theme tying the whole production together. It is a prime example of a structured format. On the other hand, "The Joe Rogan Experience," hosted by American comedian and UFC color commentator, Joe Rogan, is an example of a loose format. The episodes consist of long conversations over whiskey or weed with special guests and friends. There is no specific topic or structure to these conversations, but Rogan acts as the binding factor. The weed and alcohol play a part in adding to the brand, too.

There are other formats for podcasts aside from the basic one-person-show, co-hosted, and interview formats. These include tabletop (where hosts record themselves playing a tabletop game), improv, and panel discussions.

4. **Flexibility**

The last element that characterizes podcasts is flexibility. Podcasts come in all shapes, durations, and frequencies.

The only layout you need to stick to is the one that makes you comfortable.

An episode should last for as long as you want it to — the average length for 2021 was thirty-seven minutes and thirty seconds, but there are many podcasts, like "A Thousand Things to Talk About," that are two–three minutes an episode.

You will not be forgotten if you do not release daily. You can go daily, weekly, biweekly, or even monthly. It is all up to you and what keeps your viewers engaged.

How Do Podcast Streaming Services Work?

For Listeners

As a listener, there are many platforms through which you can gain access to all the podcasts you want: Spotify, Apple Podcasts, Google Podcasts, Stitcher, Audible, and more. All you have to do is sign up and start browsing. Do you need to pay to listen? Not always. Some of these platforms offer a paid premium version, but other than that, the platforms themselves do not charge you for browsing and listening.

However, this does not mean that the creators cannot charge you for listening. Some creators get a portion of their income from their extra features. By paying for a subscription, listeners can access additional content, like bonus episodes, interviews, and bloopers. In addition, some creators only release their content to paying subscribers.

For Creators

After uploading their content on a podcast hosting service or online server, creators can choose the platforms to which they want to send their content. These platforms then allow creators to set up their own revenue systems, which consist of free (creators get their revenue from ads rather than listeners), freemium (listeners pay for the extras), or paid (users pay to listen). What is the catch? There is not one so far.

Most platforms do not take money from the creator's revenue unless creators choose to up their revenue stream by asking for paid subscriptions. Spotify announced that, in 2023, it would start taking five percent of a creator's total subscription revenue. Meanwhile, Apple announced it would be taking thirty percent of the net revenue from creators in the first year and only fifteen percent in the following years. Nevertheless, both platforms have assured creators that their revenue from ads will remain untouched.

Do People Listen to Podcasts?

Well, in 2020, the number of podcast listeners worldwide was 485 million listeners, according to Statista. In 2019, Discover Pods stated that 82.4 percent of podcast consumers spend over seven hours per week listening. Last but not least, Edison Research stated in 2019 that 65 percent of podcast listeners do their listening on portable devices.

These numbers have increased since then, especially with the onset of the coronavirus pandemic, which caused a forty-two percent rise in global usage, according to Voxnest. It is not difficult to see the upward trend with more and more people recognizing the hidden gem of podcasts. Do not forget that the speed of life keeps getting faster, and the faster it gets, the less time people have to sit down and watch a whole show. Most would rather just listen to something on the way to work or pop on their earphones during their lunch break or even fall asleep next to the familiar voices of podcast hosts.

Downloading podcasts and listening to them online alone is enough to ramp up demand significantly.

Overall, the demand for podcasts is high and is expected to keep getting higher and higher. Thus, if you are worried you may be going into a saturated market, you don't have to worry anymore. You still need to put effort into your content because all anyone needs for a podcast is a microphone and audio-editing software, so you have to make yours stand out.

Why Would Anyone Want to Start a Podcast?

Anyone with headphones, a laptop, and something to say can start a podcast, but why would they want to? Most importantly, why are content creators willing to invest so much into their podcasts by buying better sound equipment, learning audio editing/hiring an editor, and paying for marketing costs? Well, where there is smoke, there's fire. Here is why creators are flocking toward podcasts:

The Income

Podcast creators get their revenue from three main sources:

1. Sponsorships

Companies are always looking for ambassadors and sponsors to advertise their products and contribute to their brand image. Guess whom they are always eyeing… influencers. The more credibility you have and the larger your audience, the better your chance of finding the right sponsor for you. In exchange for mentioning the company and its products, you will receive a certain amount of money/compensation depending on your contract with the brand. If you work hard enough, you can get one of your favorite companies to sponsor you.

2. Advertisements

The advertisement revenue system works similarly to YouTube videos and online blogs. You get paid depending on the number of listeners and the duration of the advertisement. According to Advertise Cast, the average pay for a thirty-second ad is eighteen dollars for every 1,000 listeners—it is called the cost per mile or CPM.

3. Subscriptions

As mentioned, creators get to control what their audience pays for, be it access to additional content, the whole podcast, or nothing at all.

Merchandise and events are also considered additional sources of income, but only for those popular enough to get people to buy their T-shirts, printed mugs, books, hoodies, etc., and attend events.

Activism

Yes, podcasts can be a form of activism. They are a mass communication medium that allows people to share their thoughts and opinions, and if you are good at engaging viewers, you can use your podcast to start a dialogue on a cause close to your heart. Civil rights activist DeRay Mckesson started his podcast, "Pod Save the People," for this exact reason.

Connecting with People

Sometimes creating is about connection, and podcasts are a great way to reach people individualyl. Unlike other media, podcasts make space for our humanity. It is a dialogue, a two-way conversation between a host and their listeners who use social media to respond.

Dialogue is how we normally show who we are to others, and just as you can form a special connection with an author after reading a book, so can listeners when they listen to their favorite host speaking in their ears for forty-five minutes.

Self-Expression

As humans, we need to self-express. Some do it through movies, some through music or writing, and others do it through talking. Podcasts allow those who best express themselves through talking to shine and fill the world with what they have to offer, be it tutorials, insightful questions, news, political insights, and the list goes on.

Education

While videos are your best bet if you want to learn about fixing a leaky pipe or how to hard reset your laptop, podcasts hit the spot when you seek knowledge on intellectual/abstract matters. Knowledge is something that many out there are thirsty for, but not everyone finds a source that speaks to them. Books work for some, but not everyone. If you're good at explaining things, you may want to consider using podcasts to talk about anything from ancient philosophical concepts to film theories.

Promoting a Brand

Brands are everywhere. Shane Dawson is a brand. Colleen Ballinger, a.k.a Miranda Sings, is a brand. Matt D'Avella is a brand. What defines a brand? It is an appearance/style or any number of features that set businesses (and, in this case, content creators) apart.
If you look at all the Apple products, you will see that they share a similar look that distinguishes them from any other tech products on the market. That is what a brand is. Now, when Apple offers its products for use in movies/series, that's promoting a brand. Many content creators and businesses use podcasts as yet another medium to promote their brands, advertise their content/products, and increase their consumer base.

Podcasting vs. Other Media

To get this out of the way, no medium is inherently better than the other. It all depends on you as a creator, your message/purpose, and your audience. In other words, podcasting could be the best medium for you but the worst medium for other creators. What we will be doing in this section is laying out the features of podcasting as a medium.

- **Low Production Costs**

Podcasting has the lowest production costs, second only to writing. All it requires is a laptop and a working Internet connection. You can start while spending almost no money, which is great. Nevertheless, the more income you make, the more you will need to up your production quality to attract advertisers and sponsors and avoid plateauing (when your audience numbers reach a point of stagnancy).

- **Demanding Writing Style**

Believe it or not, podcasts are scripted, no matter how improvised or natural they feel. They may not be scripted word for word, perhaps, but there is always an outline and some "stage directions" to guide the conversation in some way or somehow. Thus, having a script is essential.

Podcasts are fully dependent on dialogue to entertain audiences and maintain attention, so it is more demanding than writing for videos or other things. On the bright side, writing for podcasts offers much more flexibility because, once you have an outline, you are free to do whatever you want with the episode. Plus, you do not have to worry about planning for video content, only audio.

- **Ease of Consumption**

One thing that makes podcasts such a fan favorite is that they are easily consumable. They're audio files, so streaming them does not require as much data as videos. They can be downloaded for offline listening. You can also listen to them on the go, wherever you are and regardless of what you are doing. It is the entertainment industry's equivalent to a snack.

- **Limited**

When you choose podcasts as your medium, you sacrifice the appeal and potential of video-based media. Not only that, but instead of relying on clothes, makeup, facial expressions, body language, editing, camera work, and lighting to create your brand, you will have to convey everything you are through your voice, choice of words, subject matter, themes, and overall pace, as well as through the use of music.

- **Intimate and Engaging**

As a podcast creator, you will be heard through earphones by interested individuals — group listenings are not the most popular mode of podcast consumption. This one-on-one setting makes podcasts a more intimate medium. One-on-one, you can get through to your listener and get them to connect and engage with you directly. What is more, people are more likely to be responsive without anyone around because an individual is more capable of listening from a place of vulnerability when they are alone and in a safe space.

Is the Podcast Medium Right for You?

This is a brief questionnaire to help you decide whether or not investing your effort in podcasting is the right choice for you.

Do You Enjoy Talking?

As a podcast host, you will have to do a lot of talking, and not just talking, but a little voice acting, too, because it adds a little zing and keeps the flow fresh. You may also have to host people on your show, so you'll have to converse with them as well. If you love talking and expressing yourself, your ideas, and your feelings through the spoken word, podcasts are definitely right for you.

Do You Have Something to Share with the World?

You cannot get up there and ramble for ten minutes or so. Granted, it may be fun for the first few times, and people may tune in, but sooner or later, people will catch on, and they will start losing interest.

To create a successful podcast, you need to have something to say, and you need to put it into a package that grabs people's attention.

Do You Enjoy Interviewing People?

An interviewer does much more than just talk to a guest for a while. An interviewer mines their topics to bring out the best of their interviewee. They actively listen to their guest to find their next reply and question. Interviewers can make someone feel heard, seen, and comfortable enough to open up with details about their experiences. It is not a difficult job, but it requires a lot of tact and constant effort. If it's not something you enjoy, you may struggle with several podcast formats. If you find joy/excitement in interviewing people, you will have a lot of fun.

Do Your Friends Tell You that You Have a Unique Voice?

Voice is a big deal when it comes to podcasts. You do not have to sound like an angel to get people's attention, but it helps if you have a unique voice. Morgan Freeman, Emma Jones, Benedict Cumberbatch, James Earl Jones, and Samuel L. Jackson—you probably even heard their voices before you saw their faces. If you have a unique voice, you may get a lot of recognition for it, and you will definitely enjoy using your voice. Remember to take notice of other people's opinions. We all can be a little biased when it comes to our vocal skills.

Do you want to promote your brand or business but are struggling with the limits and burdens of social media marketing?

Podcasts are a great way to promote your brand, but only if you know how to do them correctly. A bad podcast will simply be a waste of time and money, and it may cost you some followers. On the other hand, a good podcast can be exactly what you need to drive audiences to your brand's socials and revive your consumer base.

Are You Quick-Witted?

If you can think on your feet and have a knack for catching details on the fly, you will love the medium, especially if you ever decide to go live. You'll find that the quickness of wit goes a long way when it comes to earning an audience's favor, whether it be from the references you use, the points you make, or the depth of the conversations you have with your guests.

Now that we have covered the basics of the podcasting world, it is time to start the creation process. What is your premise? What do you want and love to talk about? How do you want to talk about it? We will help you answer all this in-depth to help you fine-tune your concept and create your brand identity. Be sure to keep a pen and paper handy, so you can brainstorm as you read.

Chapter 2: Pinpointing Your Niche and Audience

Behind every successful podcast lies a lot of research and brainstorming. It is never as simple as coming up with an idea and jumping straight into the execution. A whole development process guarantees you a solid concept, perfect execution, an audience you can depend on, and, most importantly, enough subject matter for a constant flow of gripping episodes. This chapter's main focus is to take you through this development process. If you have not yet developed your podcast's core ideas, this chapter will give you a running start, but only if you do the work. If you have some experience and have already developed a podcast, let this chapter be your chance to fine-tune your concept and understand the factors contributing to a podcast's success.

Niche

Until you have selected your niche, your specialty, you may have difficulty imagining what your podcast will feel like and what your episodes will be about. You may have had many ideas floating around in your head, but none strong enough for you to follow through on, and that is okay. You may also have come into this chapter ready with a concept you found ground-breaking or with a few episodes/seasons below your belt, and you want to take your content to the next level. Regardless of where you are in your development process, there is something for you here.

Your niche is what your podcast will be centered upon. For Joe Rogan, it is the art of conversation. For Office Ladies' Jenna Fischer and Angela Kinsey, it's NBC's "The Office." For Stuff You Should Know Josh Clark and Charles W., it's delving deep into random topics.

As you can see, the core idea influences what the podcast is targeting as an audience, as well as the podcast's format and name. It also influences all your branding, scripts, and episodes.

An unrefined niche will leave you swimming in a sea of ideas with no specific direction, so you may end up with a podcast that has nothing to set it apart from others. However, a refined niche acts as the foundation for building a unique podcast that is *both* informative and entertaining.

Select and Refine Your Niche

Step 1: Start Big

This is the initial brainstorming phase. Your goal here is to come up with as many ideas as you can. Nothing here is off the table unless it is something you are not interested in or one that probably will not attract an audience. Consider this the beginning of the funnel; many ideas will go in, but only a few will make it to the end.

Step 2: Market Research

Now that you found some topics or areas you are interested in pursuing, it is time to see what will be the most lucrative ones and the best angle to give yourself an edge.

Market research is about checking out the competition and the audience. If your niche is highly competitive, you will try to squeeze yourself into an already saturated market. To do that, you must be prepared to work unbelievably hard, be forever consistent, and truly stand out. If, however, the competition is not intense, it means that you'll easily find your place when it comes to fulfilling your audience's wants and needs in the category you have chosen.

Knowing your audience will help you understand what they like, dislike, want, need, and which podcasts they are listening to. Then you can begin understanding the areas lacking content and start to figure out how to fill that gap in the market. You can understand your audience better through researching social media trends and talking to your potential future audience whenever you get a chance.

Step 3: How Deep Does the Well Go?

Here is where you see how much episode content you can draw from your topic. Not all topics can survive forever. Just like TV shows end when the writers have squeezed the most they could out of the story, podcasts can end when you run out of things to talk about. In addition, some ideas are easy to develop, and others are much harder. That is why it helps to have an outline that you can use to test your idea and angles.

Step 4: Expansion

The bad news no one sees coming is that, except for a few niche markets, the well does eventually dry up. Gradually, you will reach the point of being unable to mine for any more content, and that is when you'll need some fresh meat in the form of expanding your category. Some are easier to expand upon than others. A football commentary podcast, for instance, can start interviewing players to rejuvenate their audience base. Meanwhile, Joe Rogan needs to keep finding bigger and more important guests because his specialty of conversation is limited.

To find your next great expansion idea, you want to ask yourself, "Can I adopt another topic related to my original one? Can I smoothly tie it in with other topics, or is it going to look like I'm struggling?"

Once you have gone through these steps, you'll find yourself with a more detailed and precise understanding of your podcast's market and premise. Remember, good content podcasts are in demand, have a lot of content to offer, and can be leveraged into an expansion when needed.

Who Is Your Target Audience?

This is a question you will have to ask yourself over and over throughout this chapter. It will help you understand your show better and hone your ideas and overall vision as you go deeper into the brainstorming process.

Your target audience is the demographic or part of society that you believe would like your content. They are the ones you depend on for the most number of listens and engagement rates.

When Dr. Dre started Beats with Jimmy Lovine, their main target was the youth market, but more specifically, they targeted people who had the need/want to celebrate their culture. One of their most successful marketing campaigns was their first guerilla marketing campaign. The company gave its headphones to some of the Olympic athletes participating in the 2012 London summer Olympics. The company's sales increased by 116 percent as a result.

The campaign had a very specific target audience and goal. Once the marketing team set their sights on whom they wanted to influence, they could focus all their effort on that demographic.

Granted, marketing is a discipline in which you plan the methods you will use to attract your audience, so you will have to run a marketing plan in conjunction with your podcast to ensure your podcast's success. If you already have a podcast, try to reflect on the tactics you used that increased the number of listeners and why they worked. In almost all cases, you'll find that the root cause of your success was related to having a specific target audience.

In contrast, a general target audience will limit you. If you do not know whom you are talking to, how will you decide on a language and a manner of speech that suits your audience? Whom will you tailor your content toward? If your audience is too wide/general, you'll find yourself confused, frustrated, and indecisive. You'll also find your show bland and without a particular direction.

Take a moment to think about whom you want to attract with your content. Whom is it aimed at? Who do you want/expect to be listening to you on the other side?

Try to think about them in terms of:

Age Group

Is your content supposed to interest teens aged between twelve–seventeen years? Adults from ages eighteen to thirty-four? Or adults from ages thirty-five to fifty?

Of course, you are not limited to these three choices, but the point is that you should pick an age group and aim your content at it. Now, you may be wondering, "Isn't that going to make me miss out on other groups?" It could, but the fact is, you cannot please everyone.

When you become popular with a certain age group, people will naturally start flocking your way regardless. See Facebook: The product was created for young adults at their university-going age, but now it is for people of all ages.

If you have already figured out your demographic, your job is not done yet. Take a look at your current listeners and their statistics. What age group do they belong to? Have you succeeded in attracting the people you wanted to attract, or did your style find an audience elsewhere?

Answering those two questions will help you narrow down your target audience's age even more. It could also show that you need a change in style because you're not appealing to those you're after. Last but not least, it could cause you to abandon your current targeted age group and direct your effort toward a whole different market because it works better for you.

Interests

What does your audience want to know about? What interests them? True-crime stories? Book reviews? Social issues?

Why do you think they would be interested in hearing what you have to say? If, for example, your podcast revolves around food and its connection to culture, your target audience will be people who like food, culture, or both and who are interested in exploring the relationship between the two. How do you think this will affect your content? Could it make you focus more on food history than recipes? Would recipes then serve you better as bonus content for subscribers or as part of the occasional special episode where you interview a guest?

Understanding the common aspects between your interests and what your audience wants is key to developing an appealing podcast. Be sure to flesh out your audience's interests because it will help you develop your content episode by episode. Let us say that your target is university students interested in sports who happen to be primarily males. What sports are they interested in? What aspect of the sport do they like the most? Why? Would they be more interested in hearing from players and coaches than hearing from team managers?

The more details you can gather through observation and research, the more specific your content will be, and the more your audience will enjoy listening. Why wouldn't they if you are hitting all the right marks?

Ethnicity/Cultural Origins

Culture and ethnicity play a big part in the identity of your target audience. They also highly influence how you will be communicating with your audience. Each culture comes with its habits, references, traditions, beliefs, language, dialect, and history — all of which can be used to get through to your audience. Understanding one's culture, even your own, can help you to understand whom you are talking to and better communicate with them.

Each culture also has its taboos and sensitive topics. An understanding of these will help you navigate your way around sensitive issues.

Financial Status

If your podcast is dedicated to serving golfing enthusiasts, it is safe to assume that your target audience is people who can afford the luxury of regularly playing golf. This means you can comfortably set your subscription prices at certain rates without fearing that your prices are too high.

Meanwhile, if your podcast is about thrifting or surviving life on a budget, it would not really make sense for you to ask people to pay subscriptions, especially at higher rates. They are looking to save money and not spend it on yet another luxury—unless, of course, you prove yourself to be worth that money.

Gender

Podcasts oriented toward specific genders are designed to represent everything about that gender and celebrate their identity. Keep in mind that not all podcasts have to target a specific gender. However, if you would like your podcast to be centered on gender identity, you will need to specify the gender you are targeting and do some research that goes past your opinions and thoughts.

Sexual Orientation

Sexual orientation is also a big criterion that can completely change the packaging of your podcast. It makes sense that a podcast about the dating life of an asexual should be packaged in a way that another asexual finds relatable. After all, they are the main focus and not people of other sexual orientations. Keep in mind that this needs to be handled with a lot of tact as you need your podcast to represent its audience and create a sense of community while carefully staying away from any clichés.

Wants and Needs

We all have wants and needs. Wants are non-essentials that can improve your experience, but their absence will not take away from your life. Meanwhile, needs are essential. Unfulfilled needs result in horrible experiences, and they push people to seek changes. As a content creator, your job is to figure out what your target audience needs and wants out of a podcast and identify how these needs and wants have been previously fulfilled by other content creators. Once you have all the information, you can start to plan your approach.

How are you going to fulfill the audience's wants and needs? Why would an audience come to you rather than other creators?

The better you can reach an accurate picture of whom you are targeting, the better you will cater to them when it comes to your content, release frequency, and pricing structure. It may look like a complicated process, but it really is not. Finding your target audience is simple, but it requires a lot of research and mental effort. Once you have done the research, you'll have your target audience. Before moving on to the next section, remember to pick a target audience you enjoy talking to. These are the people you'll be engaging with for a very long time. You need to like them—or at least want to be a part of their community.

Format

The previous chapter discussed the many show formats; one-person shows, co-hosted shows, interviews, tabletop, improv, panel discussions, and more. As an original content creator, you get to pick the format that works best for you, your niche, resources, and skills.

One-Person Shows

Being the one host means that you will not have to share the spotlight and will have absolute control over what gets produced. However, having fewer people also means the responsibility falls solely on you to generate content. It means less creative input, and there is not anyone to balance you out when you are having a bad day. It is the best format for people who like to create without bounds and have a specific vision of what they want to achieve.

Co-Hosted Shows

They are the best for a pair of people with a lot of chemistry to go around. Granted, there is the added risk that your podcast will be at stake if your relationship with your co-host goes sour. Nevertheless, there is also the fact that you will have twice the creative input, a dynamic unique to you two, and someone you trust to give you honest feedback. If you work best in teams, you'll want to try co-hosting.

Interviews

The format is great to establish enough credibility and connections to get significant people to come on your show. Keep in mind, production costs for this format are high due to the time, energy, and money spent on getting the big names on your show.

Tabletop

A dangerous attempt unless you can guarantee that the audience will not turn away. As much as you and your friends can be fun to watch, other people may not agree. You could add alcohol or some mind-altering substance to make it fun, add special guests into the mix, or find another element that makes your tabletop game stand out. It also helps if you are already famous on the forums.

Improv

It is great, but the improvisational feel of the episode can get too old too fast. Be sure you take advantage of the flexible nature of improv and fit it within a particular context of your choosing.

Panel Discussions

The key to a successful panel discussion podcast is a good moderator. Other than that, it has the same advantages and disadvantages as a co-hosted show.

Podcast Name

Coming up with a name for your podcast is the most fun part of the whole process, and it is where you will get to experience your creativity at its best.

Your name has to meet four conditions:

1. It has to be simple.
2. It has to be memorable.
3. It has to be catchy.
4. It has to inform.

You might have noticed that every podcast name indicates a little something about the podcast, but it does so in a smooth way that gets stuck in your head. For example, "Stuff You Should Know" is very casual and simple but incredibly informative. The podcast is, in fact, casual in nature, and it revolves around stuff one should know. On the other hand, "Pod Save the People" is not as informative, but the name has a sociopolitical feel and is incredibly catchy.

With a niche, an audience, a format, and a name, you should have everything you need to move on to the next chapter. However, before you do, take a few moments to see if the niche you have selected feels right. As a creator, you must trust your intuition to guide you. How do you feel about where your podcast is standing right now?

Chapter 3: Branding and Planning Your Content

This chapter discusses how to brand your podcast and plan for content. It will go into more detail about the importance of branding before starting a podcast, what you need to do when planning your content, and some ideas on how to make your podcast stand out from the rest.

What Is Podcast Branding?

Branding a podcast means making it cohesive, recognizable, and a stand-alone entity. Your audience should be able to recognize your show within a few seconds of hearing you speak, think about the content presented in each episode, and/or see any accompanying images or media (like artwork).

Podcast branding includes everything that your audience sees or hears when it comes to the podcast. This includes artwork, logo, intro music, outro music, episode descriptions, and show notes, as well as images posted on social media about your content/show/podcast episodes, etc.

What Are Some Good Podcast Branding Examples?

There are so many great podcasts out there to choose from. Here are a few examples of high-quality branding for podcasts:

- **The Tim Ferriss Show** — This podcast has an iconic and instantly recognizable logo, artwork with bold colors and shapes representing each episode topic (which are usually listed in the show notes), intro/outro music specific to each guest that fits their personality, and even a custom typeface that is used for the show notes.
- **Freakonomics Radio** — This podcast has an easily recognizable logo with colors consistent throughout social media posts, intro music specific to each episode topic (which are usually listed in the show notes), and a custom typeface used for the show notes.

What Is Content Planning for a Podcast?

Content planning for a podcast is exactly what it sounds like: creating a plan for the content to be used to produce your show. Creating an outline before you begin recording helps ensure that each episode is cohesive and covers topics most important/relevant to your audience, which can increase engagement from listeners.

Content Planning involves brainstorming topics you want to cover, including other potential questions or thoughts that may come up during the recording process. It goes without saying that you should also plan out episodes in advance, so there is enough time to prepare your content before each show.

Now that you are familiar with the basic definitions of branding and content planning, let us tear apart these topics to discuss the nitty-gritty.

Branding Your Content

When it comes to branding your content, you need a consistent look across all platforms. This means having artwork specific to each episode and used on social media posts about the show/podcast episodes (like Facebook or Twitter). It also means having logos for both the podcast itself and any accompanying images specifically created with this brand in mind.

You also need intro and outro music specific to each episode topic. You can use royalty-free songs that you purchase from sites like Bensound, PondFive, or PremiumBeat. There are also websites where users upload their own music, which is free for others to download (like SongFreedom).

Lastly, there should be a custom typeface used specifically for the show notes. This will maintain a cohesive connection between your artwork, social media posts, and show notes.

Creating a Brand Identity

Brand identity involves delivering a consistent message to your target audience by developing niche *brand assets*. This includes the logo, color scheme, typography (typeface), and other assets used to represent your podcast visually.

The most important aspect of developing a brand identity is your value proposition. This is the promise you make to your audience about what makes them unique and why they need your content/show/podcast episodes. The value proposition statement should answer these questions:

What do you want people to believe?
\What are some common misconceptions about this topic?
Why does it matter for this target audience specifically?
How will potential listeners be part of this community?
What do you want your listeners to think or feel when they hear about or see your brand assets (logo, typeface, color scheme)? When people see the podcast artwork on social media posts or in their feed, what thoughts will go through their minds?

Once you have answered these questions, you should have a pretty good idea of your value proposition statement. For example, the Freakonomics Radio podcast's brand identity includes their name in bold orange text with a green and yellow outline to convey trustworthiness and innovation (using color psychology). When people see this logo in social media posts or show notes for episodes, it brings up thoughts related to education, knowledge, and economic thinking.

Another example is the BrainStuff podcast's band colors of bold pink, yellow, and blue. They convey power and authority through both color psychology and the boldness/strength of the design itself.

Creating Brand Assets

Brand assets are specific visual representations of your show's identity, including logo(s), color scheme, typography (typeface), and more. A podcast's brand asset bouquet should include the following:

1. Logo
2. Artwork
3. Fonts and Typeface
4. Colors
5. Graphics and Images

Logo

Your logo is the most important brand asset because it serves as your show's visual representation. It should be unique to your podcast and instantly recognizable by listeners when they see/hear about you in social media posts or on other platforms. When people look at this image, what thoughts go through their minds?

We recommend starting with a simple design that can be used for both your podcast artwork and social media posts about the show. For example, you could have a logo that is just your name in an easy-to-read font with some design elements around it (like color or texture).

It is also important to use this image across all platforms to avoid inconsistencies in your brand identity. People should know that when they see this image, it is related to you and your content.

Artwork

Your artwork is what people will immediately associate with the podcast itself. It could be a collage of images or just one photo — it just needs to visually represent all aspects of each episode topic interestingly.

When creating your artwork, you should consider what colors and shapes are most prominent in each image to represent the podcast's value proposition.

Artwork should also include some form of your logo or show name to make it instantly recognizable. You can either do these by yourself or hire an artist to do it for you.

Fonts and Typeface

The font used should be easy to read, both in color (is this type of font the same on white/black background?) and the lettering style itself. You can either use your logo or show name for this, so people know when they see this font, it is related to you and your content.

Selecting a font that is easy to read means that people can actually read and see what you are saying. It also makes your show notes look more professional and well put together, positively contributing to how listeners perceive the content itself.

The font of your podcast should align with your theme. For example, use a serious font like Georgia for a political podcast.

You can easily find fonts online for free, but make sure they are high quality and easy to read.

Tools for finding the right font include Adobe Fonts, Font Squirrel, DesignModo Fonts, Google Fonts, etc.

You will want to select a set of fonts that work in harmony with each other. Typically, you will need a font for the title, sub-title, body font, and show notes. A font combination generator tool (easily available online) is a great way to find the best font combination for your podcast.

Colors and Shapes

Colors are a vital component of brand identity since they are what people will immediately associate with the podcast itself. You can use color psychology to convey different meanings depending on what colors you choose.

Your brand should have a set of primary colors (usually three colors) that you will use the most. These are your "brand colors."

You can also have secondary colors (usually less than three) that complement your brand and may be used sparingly in select circumstances.

The same goes for shapes—not all brands should use them, but they can add an extra style element to your podcast when used properly.

Avoid using too many colors or shapes in your artwork, which can be hard on the eyes and distracting.

Graphics and Images

Every image you include should have a purpose, whether it is to tell the story of your podcast or enhance an element in the artwork.

You may also want to use graphics for various places around your show notes (like headers) so they are consistent across all platforms. Using images that align with each episode topic can help listeners better understand what is being discussed.

If you have a list of episodes, using the same image at the top can help people quickly identify what each episode is about. This also makes it easier for listeners to browse through your archive and find topics they are interested in.

A great way to do this is by compiling screenshots from past episodes that fit well together in a collage. Avoid overusing any one image or graphic since it can be boring and repetitive to viewers.

Use free online tools, such as Canva and Pablo, to create images that fit your brand.

Formats for Images

When looking at image dimensions, it is important to remember the various devices from which people will be listening to/watching your podcast—including laptops, iPhones, Android phones, tablets, etc.

Backgrounds and Patterns

The background of your artwork can be used to get viewers' attention but should not overpower the content itself. Sometimes it is best to use a simple white or light gray background so that people focus on what you are saying rather than images in the background (which may vary depending on the device).

Solid colors, patterns, and textures give the artwork a more professional look than using an image as your background.

Remember that you want people to quickly see what is being presented in front of them so they can focus on listening/watching!

Banner Size

For websites like iTunes and WordPress, where you will be embedding your show notes, make sure your artwork is at least 1400 x 1400 pixels in size (for iTunes) or 800 x 800 (for WordPress).

Image File Format

Your image should be saved as a JPEG. If possible, upload an image with the PNG extension instead of converting to another file format since it will retain its quality better than when converted.

Creating Thumbnails

Every time you upload a new episode, it is essential that your podcast artwork is updated to reflect the latest information. A good way to do this is to create a thumbnail for each episode to inform listeners what they are listening to on their devices.

You can use the same format for your episode thumbnails as you did in your full artwork for brand consistency, but it's important to remember that they should be much smaller. A thumbnail should include:

- Your episode name and number (or word count).

- The main image of your artwork.
- A background color or pattern that is complementary to the colors in your brand's primary palette. If you do not have a set palette, it would be best for the background to remain white/gray so that people can focus on the text.
- In the bottom left corner, include a compelling tagline that is brief and descriptive of your podcast episode content. This should be in all caps, so it stands out from other elements on the page.
- Use white text for this area instead of switching to another color since it will help people quickly understand what you are promoting.
- Don't forget to include links to your website, social media accounts (Twitter and Facebook), iTunes, Spotify, etc.

Creating an Avatar

You can also use your artwork to create an avatar for yourself, especially if you are the podcast host. This will make it easier for people to recognize you when listening to your podcast.

When designing an avatar, keep these points in mind:

- Your photo should be a clear and high-quality image. If you struggle with this, it may help to ask someone else to take the picture for you so they can frame your face in the best way possible.
- Keep your avatar's size at about 200 x 200 pixels, as that is what most platforms will recognize when associating your avatar with your podcast.
- Use a contrast color (like white or black) for any text and central image to help them stand out from one another.
- As far as possible, avoid text in your avatar since it will take away from the central image.

Planning Your Content

Content is central to the success of your podcast, so be sure to plan it out before recording. What are you going to cover in your podcast? Who is the intended audience for this particular episode? How can you make it easy and convenient for listeners/watchers to access all available episodes without them getting frustrated by not finding what they want and possibly losing interest?

Here are a few important points that will help you plan your content:

- Ask yourself what kind of podcast this will be. Is it a comedy, general information, an interview show? What is the main purpose behind making these podcasts, and who are they for?
- Your planning must include any major points you want to cover in each episode within your podcast's planned time (90-120 minutes).
- Your content should also include a call to action for each episode, whether it is directly related to the topic or not. This could encourage people to subscribe and/or contact you with questions or comments about what they have heard so far.
- Make sure your scripts are written in a conversational tone since it will help people feel like they are listening to a friend and not someone who is reading from a script.
- Do not forget to include important details such as your website address, social media profiles (Facebook/Twitter), iTunes link, etc., so listeners can easily access all available podcast episodes or other relevant content.
- Make sure you have an intro and outro for each episode in your series to introduce yourself, your topic/focus, and explain what listeners can expect from this particular episode. You also need to state why it is important or relevant today (use storytelling techniques here!), how they will benefit from listening/watching the content in this episode, and why they should share your podcast with others.
- Your intro/outro should be no longer than thirty seconds, as most people will start listening to a new episode as soon as it begins playing on their device, especially if you are hosting the podcast or appearing in each episode. If they have to wait more than a minute for something interesting to happen, they may get bored and choose to skip it.
- Your intro needs to be catchy enough that listeners want to hear more of your podcast (if you are hosting or speaking in each episode), yet not too long that people are not interested at the end.

Always make sure you are providing value to your audience without asking for anything in return. People who listen to podcasts do it because they enjoy the content and want more of this type of information/entertainment, not necessarily because they expect something from you or feel like they "owe" it to you. However, if someone enjoys what you are doing, it is okay to ask them if they would like to support the podcast with a donation or paid subscription.

Designing a Podcast Script

Designing a script for your podcast is a vital step toward creating quality content. It should be written in the same way you naturally speak, even if it is just one person like yourself (in this case).

- Use conversational language and avoid overly formal words or phrases that might sound unnatural when spoken out loud (such as using the word "utilize" when you really mean "use").
- Include stories, examples, analogies, and metaphors to help listeners understand what you are explaining in your podcast. This can also keep people engaged throughout each episode instead of having them tune out after a few minutes because it is not relevant or interesting enough for them at that moment.
- Use the word "you" as much as possible since it will help people feel more connected to your content and keep them engaged.
- Incorporate humor/jokes in your anecdotes or stories, especially for those who enjoy comedy podcasts. This makes you come over as a personable host with whom listeners will want to connect.
- Make sure you have a clear script outline before recording, so there are no awkward pauses or dead ends. This can be beneficial for those who may not understand what is being said otherwise, especially if the podcast does not include any visuals to help explain it further.
- Allow time for testing and practicing this script with other people to see how it sounds or flows, and then tweak certain parts to make sure everything makes sense.
- The outline should be no longer than a paragraph in length since listeners will tune out if they are not interested at the end of this section. If there is additional information that needs to be included at the beginning of each episode (such as an intro or outro), that can be included in the script as well.

Here is a basic podcast template example:

"Hi! Welcome to (Podcast Name). I'm your host (your name), and today we're talking about...

<Intro Music>

"(insert theme of the episode here). We will discuss what this means for you today, why it's important or relevant now more than ever before, how you can benefit from listening/watching this podcast in particular, and then finally, I'll give you some pointers if you would like to learn more or start doing xxx straight away. To get the most out of today's episode, have paper and a pen handy, or record this podcast so you can refer back to it later on.

"Before we begin, here are a few things related to today's topic that you might enjoy or find helpful."

- At the end of each episode, make sure to include a call-to-action (CTA) for your listener by asking them what they learned from listening and how it can be applied in their lives. You could also ask if anyone would like to contribute feedback, share an experience, ask a question, etc.
- Be sure to highlight your guest's or co-host's name before they speak so that listeners can realize who is talking. If you are the only one speaking throughout an episode except for the CTA at the end, simply mention your name first instead of leaving it out completely. This can be beneficial if the person speaking does not have a large social media presence or is relatively unknown in the industry.

<Outro Music>

Branding and planning your content for a podcast are two of the most important factors to consider before you begin recording. The more well-thought-out and planned these qualities are, the better quality podcasts you will produce.

From branding yourself or your show on social media platforms like Twitter or Facebook to knowing exactly what type of episodes you want to produce each week (i.e., interview-style vs. educational), there is an extensive list that you need to consider beforehand to keep listeners tuning in to every single episode. It is always good practice to plan for any mishaps so everything goes smoothly during the actual process itself.

Chapter 4: Podcasting Equipment for All Budgets

Starting a podcast can be overwhelming because there are so many things to consider and remember. There is the technical stuff, and then there are all the topics you want to talk about. On top of all that, you have to decide what equipment you need to use for recording your podcast. However, the good news is that when it comes to equipment, quality is relative. You do not need the most expensive microphone to have a good-sounding podcast, but if you are just starting, chances are you want something affordable.

This chapter will explore the equipment used for podcasting. It will first discuss the absolute basics, like software and microphones. Then it'll provide some options for beginner podcasters and what you can get if you want to start podcasting on a more advanced level.

Items Needed When Starting a Podcast

To have a successful podcast, consider these items when you are on the go.

1. Smartphone Camera

The quality of smartphone cameras has improved incredibly in recent years—and you can use them for more than just taking selfies or pictures of your food. They make great podcasting tools because they can be used to record both audio and video, giving listeners the best of both worlds. Plus, most smartphones can record up to three hours of video, which is plenty for a full podcast. You can also upload the files directly to sites like YouTube, which is probably the first place where your audience will be looking for you.

2. Laptop or Tablet

Some may argue against using a laptop or tablet as podcasting equipment because some high-quality machines will give you better quality audio. However, these machines can be incredibly useful if you travel a lot or are always on the go.

Because editing software takes up a good amount of space, consider getting an external hard drive if you have a laptop with little built-in storage. If you are fine with your audio being compressed during the uploading process, you can use cloud services like Dropbox to send audio files directly to your podcasting host.

3. Phone Cord and Charger

You may think this is a given, but you would be surprised how easy it is to forget some of the essentials when you are running around. Outlets for charging your phone are not always available, so carrying a cord can keep you connected, which is important for uploading episodes after they are recorded.

4. Pen and Paper

Those who prefer to take notes by hand can use the pen and paper combo whenever inspiration strikes. It is also useful in an emergency when you may need to leave your recording equipment behind but still want to jot down information that you want to talk about later. It's also a good idea to keep a list of topics you want to cover or a calendar of when guests are scheduled for recording.

5. A Microphone

Not every podcaster needs studio-quality audio, but it is important to consider the type of podcast you want to produce and how professional it sounds. If you plan to have guests on your podcast, you will need a microphone that does not make them sound like they are sitting in the next room.

If you want to record from anywhere and do not have access to a professional recording studio, all you need is a microphone small enough to fit on your desk or in your bag. If you value audio quality and like the idea of recording in a studio, you'll need professional microphones and cables to connect them.

6. Headphones

It is important to have headphones to hear everything as you are recording your podcast. They also come in handy when you want to listen for any background noise or edits that need to be made after the recording process.

You do not need professional equipment to create an entertaining podcast that people will enjoy. However, many podcasters would argue that having at least one of these items can help you get the best quality audio possible. No matter your budget, there are options out there for all kinds of equipment.

You can purchase items like table mics and studio-quality headphones online or in some office supply stores. Also, visit websites like Craigslist or eBay to find deals on used equipment.

7. Portable USB Recorder

A portable USB recorder can be used in place of a smartphone, and it provides better quality than your phone's built-in microphone could ever deliver. They are very easy to use, and the sound quality is excellent, particularly if you plan to have guests on your podcast.

If you want a multi-track recording system, record each audio source on a separate track and then edit it in post-production. It is also possible to use an external recorder that works with your console or mixer if you do not wish to use the microphone input on your computer.

8. Mixer

Having a mixer allows you to control the sound levels of each audio source, which is preferable for some podcasters if they do not want to mess with editing different tracks. It also provides additional options that you may not have access to if using other equipment or software.

9. Microphone Stands and Shock Mounts

When it comes to setting up your studio, you will need stands and mounts that can hold your microphones in place so they do not pick up everything that is going on around them. You may also want to use external shock absorbers or sleeves if your mics tend to pick up unwanted sounds.

10. A Podcasting Host

A podcast hosting service is a great way to share your audio files with listeners, and many companies offer affordable plans for those who may not have much money to spend. This way, you can upload your podcasts from anywhere without worrying about bandwidth or storage limits. To avoid being sued for copyright infringement, do not forget to have your guests sign an agreement before you start recording.

If you want to keep things simple and old-fashioned, all of this equipment can be replaced with a computer and any kind of recording software, like GarageBand or Audacity. You will then need to record directly into your software without any hardware, as it can be difficult to edit audio properly if you are using multiple tracks. Although these tools and equipment may seem like a lot to purchase for those just getting started with recording, they will come in handy for future episodes and provide better quality than your computer's built-in microphone alone.

Equipment for Beginners

Speakers — Monitors vs. Headphones

It is important to consider the type of speakers you are using when editing your podcast after the recording process. If you are listening to your audio through headphones, it will sound different because they have a built-in equalizer that boosts bass frequencies. As a result, if you hear your voice sounding thin and high-pitched, it's actually due to the speakers rather than the mic. If you hear a lot of bass in your low end while listening through speakers, it's because they do not have a built-in equalizer that boosts vocal frequencies as headphones do.

If you are using studio monitors to listen to your podcast, it's important to make sure they are placed properly in your workspace. If you place them too far away from the wall behind them, the sound will be very thin and high-pitched. Also, if they face walls or other surfaces that reflect sound directly back at them, their high end will become more prominent. It is best if they are placed in the middle of the room, away from any reflective surfaces.

Studio headphones are perfect if you want to focus on your podcast without being distracted by outside sounds. The only thing that might interfere is if there is a lot of bass coming out of your speakers or computer, which is why it's also important to have good-quality, bass-reducing headphones to use in addition to your studio monitors.

Microphones — Dynamic vs. Condenser

Dynamic microphones are the most commonly used for podcasting because they do not require phantom power and can be plugged into your console or computer's input without any additional equipment. They come in different sizes, so you need to find something small and unobtrusive that will fit next to your monitor. That way, it will not take up too much room on your desk, and you can still access the controls easily as you record.

Condenser mics require batteries or a separate power source to work, but they can also do more than dynamic microphones because they have a wider range. This means that they pick up every little sound from your surroundings, including those pesky vocals from your speakers. It is important to have as much control as possible over the sounds you are recording, so look for a microphone with a windsock and sturdy shock mount to prevent any unwanted noises or feedback.

Proximity Effect

You should avoid having the mic too close to your mouth, or you will get excessive bass frequencies, also known as the proximity effect. If these are not reduced in editing, they will be distracting and hard to understand. You need to place your microphone at a comfortable distance so that it records only what you are saying without capturing all of the surrounding sounds.

Microphone Accessories

Windsock — Keeps the popping noises that come from breathing into your mic at bay, and it will not damage your microphone like foam or plastic covers might. You can also use the cover to protect the mic when transporting it in its carrying case.
Shock Mount — Prevents vibrations from reaching sensitive equipment by isolating the microphone from any surface it is placed on.
XLR Cable — This is used to connect professional microphones to audio equipment, and they have a screw that allows for secure connections. These cables are more durable than most other options, so they can last you a long time if you take care of them.
Headphone Extension Cord — Useful if you want to work in headphones, but your console or mixer is far away.
Headphone Adapter — This will convert one 1/4 inch jack into two 1/8 inch jacks, which allows for separate headphone and microphone connections simultaneously. This is useful if you want your guest and co-host to use headphones during the recording.
Headphone Amplifier — This is useful if you want more control over volume and quality than your computer can provide. It also allows for different connections, such as USB or XLR, which might be necessary depending on your equipment. Many headphone amps also have balanced inputs and outputs to reduce noise interference between the headphones and the console.
Portable Recorder — Do you want to make high-quality audio files but do not have a computer that lets you record into an editing program easily? A portable recorder is another option that will let you record into your device anywhere it has recording capabilities. It may not be as convenient, but it is a good solution for people who want better quality than what their phone can provide.
Microphone Stands — A microphone stand allows you to easily adjust the height of your microphone, which is important if you are recording in different locations or have multiple hosts that come into your studio often. You will also have more control over the microphone if it is on a stand since you can quickly adjust the position or angle. A good stand will accommodate desktop mics and mic stands with booms.

Equipment for Pro Podcasters

Digital Audio Workstation (DAW) — This is the computer program you will use to edit all of your audio files.
Audio Interface — This goes between your console and any other equipment that does not have a digital connection, such as microphones or headphones. It converts analog signals into digital ones to be recorded into your DAW.

Digital Recorder — This records high-quality audio files while mixing your podcast in a digital program. You can add sound effects and music, plus record any conversations or voiceovers with guests on the show. It is very helpful if all of the connections from various microphones, instruments, and other equipment can be routed through it to make recording easier.

Monitors — These are speakers or headphones that will let you listen to your recording as you make any changes and help ensure the quality is good enough before releasing your podcast.

Condenser Microphones — These are a good fit for most studio situations because they record a wide range of frequencies with clarity. They need power to work, such as from a microphone preamp or an audio interface.

Dynamic Microphones — Used for close-range, high gain applications, such as recording instruments, interviews, and voiceover, they will give you great sound quality but usually require a separate mixer or microphone port on your audio interface to work well.

Stands and Booms — These will help you attach a microphone or headphones wherever convenient.

Pop Filters — These reduce popping sounds from vocal plosives by diffusing the air pressure created by the sound waves.

Headphone Distribution Amplifier — If you have more than one headphone user, this amplifier will allow them all to listen to your recording with an equalized mix of all the speakers or content playing. This way, they can help monitor your recording without you losing the ability to listen and talk simultaneously.

Speaker Management System — This will allow listeners using various devices, such as smartphones, computers, and tablets, to listen in on your recording and send in questions to be answered during the show.

Headphone Amplifiers — Headphone amplifiers provide a dedicated audio signal to headphones so they can be used independently of other speakers or content that is playing. You will need them if you have more than one headphone user, such as a co-host, who needs to hear the show at a different volume level.

Big Ben — This disables your Internet connection automatically, so you can do any necessary audio processing without the risk of your guests or co-hosts talking over each other. It can also reduce errors in recordings, such as echo or feedback loops, by preventing you from interrupting anything playing through your speakers at a crucial moment.

One thing that is essential for any podcaster is an external microphone or two. This will give you better quality audio recorded onto your computer than using the microphones built into most desktop computers. Most people will plug their microphones directly into their computers through either a USB or an XLR port, but you can also use third-party hardware to do this.

If you are planning to bootstrap your podcast, the equipment you have available will largely determine what you can do. However, even if you are just starting with a bare minimum of podcasting gear, it is still possible to create an amazing show that sounds great. With a little bit of creativity, you are sure to make the absolute most out of your equipment.

Chapter 5: Recording Your First Podcast

Recording a podcast can be quite simple if you know what you are doing. The trick is to make sure the sound quality of your voice is crystal clear and that the microphone has been set up properly. Regardless of whether you're using your computer or an external digital recorder, there are a few basic things you need to know before you begin recording. This chapter will go over the steps to record a successful and quality podcast.

The Basics of Audio Recording

Audio recording requires more than just pressing a button on your computer. Audio must be properly recorded and then compressed into an MP3 file that can be easily published online or shared with others. There is some terminology to learn before you begin:

Bit Rate — This setting determines the quality of the audio you record. The higher the bit rate, the better quality you will have on your finished product. However, this results in larger file sizes.

Codec — A codec is simply an audio format. There are numerous codecs, but the most popular for use online is MP3.

Bit Depth — The bit depth helps determine how accurately your recording will translate. A higher bit depth means better quality.

File Format — This is the format of your finished product. The most common file formats for podcasting are MP3, WAV, and AIF.

Sample Rate — Sample rate refers to how often a sound wave is sampled when recorded and processed. The more samples, the better quality you will have in your recording.

Hardware and Software Options

A few pieces of equipment are needed to record your first podcast. A computer and digital audio recorder are your two main tools for recording a podcast. Most laptops come with built-in mics, but if your recording environment lacks a bit in the audio quality department, it is time to invest in a quality microphone. A computer is required, but it can be done without external hardware if the only goal is to publish the finished recording online or send it to others. However, there are some benefits to using an external digital recorder instead of relying on your computer's built-in microphone.

Computer — A computer is used to record the audio and then compress it into an MP3 file for distribution or storage on your website or social media accounts.

Recording Software — No recording software is required for your computer if you only share the final product with others, but some will work in conjunction with your digital recorder. If you're using a built-in computer microphone, recording software will help adjust the settings to optimize its performance.

External Digital Recorder — There are several handheld digital recorders on the market designed for use by podcasters. The two types are USB and analog. A USB recorder uses an XLR input that allows it to connect directly to your computer for recording, while an analog recorder needs to be connected via a cable. Once the audio is recorded, the digital recorder can compress the file into an MP3 or other codec of your choice.

Microphone — The microphone captures your voice and records it as an audio file. Podcasters generally use USB microphones or XLR if they are using the external digital recorder, but some small analog microphones plug directly into your computer or digital recorder.

Room — You may not think of this as an important recording tool, but it is! The room you record in will affect the quality of your sound. A room with soundproofing will reflect less noise and create a more professional-sounding podcast.

Soundproofing — Some podcasters invest in soundproofing equipment to improve their final product. A few items that can help are acoustic foam panels, which you attach directly to the walls of your recording space, or portable vocal booths, which are similar to how you would imagine a vocal booth—small and soundproof—but portable.

Podcast Software — You can record your podcast straight from your computer using dedicated software or a cloud service. Several apps on the market make it simple to try recording a podcast, such as Anchor.

There are numerous free or paid software options to record your podcast. If you are using a digital recorder, make sure it is compatible with your chosen software. Here are some of the most popular recording apps for computers and mobile devices:

Anchor — This is one of the easiest ways to try out creating a podcast. It allows you to record on the go with its mobile apps, or you can use the Anchor website to create a recording directly from your computer.

Google Voice — This is an easy way to record your podcast via Google's servers. You simply open up the chat section in Gmail and click on "record." From here, you can record directly to Google's servers and access the finished product in an MP3 file.

GarageBand — This is a great option for podcasters looking for more robust software with several features. GarageBand allows you to create podcasts through your computer or an iOS mobile app. Like Anchor, you can record your podcast directly via a computer or mobile device, but GarageBand has the added benefit of allowing you to edit the recording before the final product.

Audacity — It is free, and it works! Audacity is a popular option for podcasters because it does not come with any restrictions on your finished product. It allows you to use your microphone, recording software, and digital recorder to create an MP3 file.

Libsyn — This is one of the most common options for podcasters looking to publish their podcast on iTunes. Libsyn offers its suite of mobile recording apps and tools for hosting your audio files online.

Other Notable Apps — There are several other apps on the market that you may want to check out, such as Zencastr and Cast. In general, they all offer some type of free version with paid upgrades.

Podcast Recording Tips

There are several important aspects to keep in mind when recording your podcast. Do not worry; it is not as difficult as you think! Here are some tips for getting started:

1. **Prepping Your Digital Recorder**

You can simply use the recorder's built-in microphone or connect an external mic if you have one. Generally, if you have an XLR connector, you can simply connect your microphone to the digital recorder. If you are using a USB microphone or plugging it directly into your computer, make sure it has a built-in preamp to amplify your voice. You can set the input level of your microphone in your device's settings to avoid that loud humming or distorted sound.

2. Setting Up Your Space

The sound in your recording space will affect the final product, so it is important to make sure you are using a quiet and well-insulated room free from potential noise and reverb. If you're recording in a small closet or inside your home office, it would be wise to soundproof the room by closing and locking doors and windows to lessen any echoes. It may also help to invest in acoustic panels for any open walls.

3. Microphone Placement

When placing your microphone, avoid popping sounds by pointing your nose away from the mic and keeping your mouth at least one inch away. It is also important that you do not block or cover up the microphone with your hand, clothing, or hair, or else this will result in choppy audio quality. Make sure you place it about two to three inches away from your mouth.

4. Testing Your Digital Recorder

There are a few ways to test out your digital recorder before starting the actual recording session, including using the voice memo app built into most smartphones or making extra phone recordings in case you forget something important during your recording session. You can also record an entire episode on your digital recorder before starting the actual recording session. This will allow you to identify any potential issues with your setup or technology before it is too late.

5. Setting Your Recording Levels

Typically, when recording on your digital recorder, there are three different recording levels to choose from: low, medium, or high. You want to make sure you choose the best option for your voice. Generally speaking, if you are starting and need to practice your podcasting skills, it is recommended that you start with the lower level. This will cut out any distortion and allow you to identify any background noises that should not be there.

6. Create Your Intro and Outro

If you are using Audacity, it helps to create an intro and outro for your podcast, so your listeners feel more involved with the episode. You can include music or sounds relevant to the discussion topic, which brings the podcast to life. It also makes it seem less like a one-sided conversation. People will want to tune into your next episode because they will feel invested in your content.

7. Using an External Microphone

If you do not have a digital recorder with your built-in microphone, it is time to invest in one! There are several different microphones available depending on your budget and needs. You can purchase an inexpensive USB microphone or go for the higher-end models, which offer better sound quality, more features, and better clarity. Make sure it includes a preamp for no distortion or humming.

8. **Recording Your Voice**

When recording your voice, you must take a deep breath before speaking into the microphone. You want to start by saying your name and then get right into the content of what you are about to say. If possible, try to speak at a normal pace and avoid going too fast. You can always go back and edit your audio if need be, but the goal is to get it right from the start by bringing out your best performance.

9. **Editing Your Voice**

One of the easiest ways to edit your voice is to use an audio application that allows you to cut and delete parts of the audio file in question. Make sure you listen closely for any background noises or potential mistakes, such as stutters or silent intervals, which can be removed by simply highlighting them with your cursor. If you make any mistakes with your wording, you can easily go back into the audio file and re-record the section in question.

10. **Checking for Audio Quality**

Check your audio quality before you start uploading your podcast. This is the only way to make sure it sounds professional with no background noises or other feedback issues. You can use an online audio application like Audacity to take a snippet of your voice recording and play it back, which allows you to hear the audio in its raw form.

11. **Transcribing Your Podcast**

If you cannot afford a transcriptionist, several different software applications allow you to transcribe your audio file using your computer or laptop. You can then copy and paste it into an email, which will make it easier for others to read.

12. **Uploading Your Podcast**

When you have your final copy ready, you must upload your podcast to various directories like iTunes and Stitcher Radio. These are great places to promote your podcast across social media platforms and search engines, making it much easier for people to find your content! You can also upload your podcast to YouTube and use it as an audio track for any videos you place on the platform.

13. **Promoting Your Podcast**

The best way to promote your podcast is by making multiple accounts across various social media platforms like LinkedIn, Twitter, Facebook, Tumblr, Pinterest, etc. Each profile should be customized according to what your podcast is about and what you will be sharing with your audience. Promote it by asking relevant bloggers, celebrities, or colleagues if you can interview them on your upcoming podcast episode, which will help increase awareness for this content.

14. Recording Your Second Podcast

This time you should do something different! You can always try recording at a different time of the day or experiment with a few different microphones and recording software. The important thing is to come up with new topics and ideas so that you can help your audience grow and learn something new each time they tune in.

15. Other Recording Methods

If you do not have the space or money for a traditional digital recorder, there are a few other ways to record your voice. One way is by using a voice recorder application on your smartphone that lets you record and save files on the device itself. You can then upload these audio files manually or use a USB cord to copy them onto your computer for editing.

There are not many options when it comes to recording your voice. You can use a traditional digital recorder like the Zoom H4N, but make sure to get one with external microphones that help capture your voice more clearly and without any outside interference or background noise.

As far as recording software is concerned, you can use Audacity, which is completely free and works on both Mac and PC operating systems. It allows you to record, edit, and manipulate audio files, but make sure your computer can handle it because it needs a decent amount of processing power (RAM & CPU), especially if you plan to do some heavy editing.

Another application that is also free is Adobe Audition, which is more complex than Audacity and will take some time to get used to. This application allows you to record, upload, and promote your podcast, making it easier than ever before!

Additional Recording Tips

Some other things to keep in mind:
- Make sure you are recording in a quiet environment with as little background noise as possible because the last thing you want is for your listeners to hear feedback from your microphone.
- When it comes to hardware, make sure all your cables and connectors are working properly. This will prevent many headaches when it comes to editing.

- Before recording anything, you should always test your audio equipment to ensure there are no problems with the sound levels and quality. A great way to do this is by either speaking or playing some music from your computer speakers, which will help you identify any issues.
- When it comes to editing, you should always remove any pauses or breaks because this may cause your audience to lose interest and want to tune out early. This is done automatically in Adobe Audition or a similar application.
- Anything that does not add value to your podcast should be removed or cut down. It can be hard to let go of some content that you feel is important, but at the end of the day, your audience will love you for keeping them entertained and informed like never before!

If you are a first-time podcaster, it is important to know that recording your first podcast does not have to be difficult. All you need is a computer, some audio equipment, and the proper software application to get started. Once you do this, your main goal will be to experiment with different ideas until you find something that works best for your audience to grow and learn together. Remember, you're not alone in this! Many other podcasters are always looking for feedback from the community, so make sure to connect with them whenever possible.

Chapter 6: Editing and Post-Production

The audio for your podcast episode is recorded, and now it needs to be edited and post-produced. You have options to self-edit, use an app, or hire a freelancer or agency to do the editing for you. This can be a time-consuming process, but your podcast episode needs to be perfect for your listeners.

What are the options? What is each option best suited for? How much time and money will it cost you? This chapter will help you decide what is best for your podcast.

Self-Editing

Let us say that your recording equipment, recording space, and microphone are all optimized, but the finished product still does not sound quite right. All of this can be done by you and the use of some computer software. The time it will take to edit depends on how many mistakes you want to fix. If the changes are simple, it should not take too long to edit your audio file. If there are many errors in your recording and you want the errors to be fixed perfectly, this will take more time than editing out just one or two mistakes.

What Kind of Task Is It Best Suited For?

Since editing your podcast is best done by yourself, it is more suited for people who are experts in audio recording. You will have a better idea of what you want the final product to sound like and how to achieve that. Also, you'll quickly find errors with their recordings because they are familiar with their voices and talking style. It's best for when you want to do in-depth editing on your own.

What Are the Costs?

The price of self-editing can vary depending on how in-depth you want the editing process to be. All you need to do is invest in some computer software that will do the job for you. There are many different types of audio-editing software, including Adobe Audition, Logic Pro X, and GarageBand. Whatever software you use will need to be compatible with your computer. You can find many editing tutorials online to help you use your audio-editing software.

The Process

The process for self-editing will vary depending on the computer software you have. If you do not have any editing software, you can purchase some. There are quite a few options to choose from depending on your computer platform (Mac or PC). For example, if you are using a Mac, there is iMovie and GarageBand. If you're using a PC, there's Windows Movie Maker and Audacity. All of these are relatively easy to use so that beginners can understand how they work.

You can also look online for tutorials on how to use the software. Many people have created tutorials on YouTube that you can watch to learn how to edit out mistakes just by using your voice. You will find tutorials on how to use any editing software and computer platform. With the help of these tutorials, you can edit out your mistakes quickly and efficiently.

Pros of Self-Editing

The pros of self-editing are that it costs nothing if you have the right equipment and software and takes much less time to edit out a few simple mistakes. If there is only one or two re-recordings or little background noise, this would be a great option for editing. It is also a great option if you do not have the money to hire someone to edit your podcast episode.

Cons of Self-Editing

The cons of self-editing are that it can take a long time to edit out more than one or two mistakes and takes much concentration and time. This is not ideal for editing out complex mistakes and/or background noise. If you have to re-record more than just a few words, this is not the best option for the job.

Using an App

If you do not have the time to self-edit, using an app is a great option. Many apps are designed specifically for editing podcast audio files. All you have to do is simply upload the audio file to the app, and they will take care of editing out your mistakes. Most apps also offer a high-quality background noise filter to remove any unwanted sounds. This is especially convenient if your topic is ever-changing, like news or sports, since new stories may come up and you don't have time to edit your podcast.

What Kind of Task Is It Best Suited For?

Using an app is best suited for anyone who needs a quick and easy fix for their podcast audio file. Many people use these apps to fix mistakes they may have made during recording. This can also be helpful for quickly editing out background noise since you do not have to purchase extra equipment. Also, you can upload your file quickly and easily.

What Will It Cost?

These apps are designed to help fix any mistakes with your podcast audio files. Since they are already set up to do this, they do not cost anything extra. However, most apps will offer a monthly or yearly subscription for more advanced features. The subscriptions prices will vary depending on the app. Many of these apps are cheap or even free. The one drawback is the quality of the finished product. After using an app, your podcast audio file may still need to be edited. This means that you will have to spend more time and energy on the process.

This option costs money depending on what app you choose. You may also have to deal with some ads that the apps include, but this is usually just an initial fee and not a recurring cost. The one benefit of using an app instead of editing your audio file yourself is that it will save you time and energy.

The Process

Using an app is relatively easy if you are just looking for a quick fix for your podcast audio file. Most of these apps are designed simply to edit out mistakes and background noise without much effort. You can usually upload your file, make changes that you need to make, and then download your finished product within minutes.

The only drawback is the quality of the finished product. If you do not edit out errors before uploading your podcast to an app, this could lead to a lower-quality audio file. The app will automatically do its best to edit out your mistakes, but it may not be perfect. You will need extra equipment and tools if you want the highest possible quality for your podcast audio file. Here are the common steps to using most apps:

1. *Upload Your File* — Most apps will have a section for uploading your file. They may even give you an option to connect your Dropbox account with their software. You can upload your file directly to their site or through Dropbox.

2. *Make Changes* — Some apps will allow you to make changes (like adjusting the volume, deleting mistakes, and adding background noise filters when necessary.) These are usually easy-to-use buttons that guide you where you need to go to make changes.

3. *Select Your Edits* — You will select all of the edits you have made to your podcast audio file. The app will then put it all together and create a finished product that may need a little bit of tweaking before you are ready to upload it to your media host or website.

4. *Download Your File* — Once you have made all the changes you want, download your file to your computer. You can usually download it from the app or through a shared link.

5. *Edit Your File & Upload* — This is when you will need to edit your file. You can do this with Audacity or any other popular audio-editing software. Once you have finished editing, upload your file so that everyone can hear it.

Pros of Using an App

The biggest advantage of using an app instead of editing your podcast audio file yourself is that it saves you time and energy. You can quickly make edits to your file without having to spend much time learning how to use the software, downloading a bunch of equipment, or purchasing high-quality tools. All you need is an app and a Dropbox account.

Cons of Using an App

The biggest downside to using an app is the quality of your final product. If you do not edit out any mistakes before uploading your file, this could lead to poor sound quality in your podcast. The app does its best to edit out background noise, but it will not be perfect. Sometimes the only thing to do is get your hands on extra equipment and tools.

Outsourcing to a Freelancer or Company

Depending on the size and scale of your podcast and audience, you may want to hire a freelancer or company to edit and post-produce it. Although this can end up being more expensive, it will likely save you time and energy in the long run. Once you find a freelancer or company you want to work with, they will usually send you an estimate based on the length of your podcast file and other factors. These estimates may vary depending on how many revisions they need to do. The company or freelancer will usually give you an all-inclusive price, so there will be no added fees once the project is finished.

Once you get your estimate, review it. If it seems too high, you should go to another company or freelancer and get a comparative quote. You may also want to consider cutting back on the amount of work you want them to do.

What Kind of Task Is It Best Suited For?

Although you can edit your podcast audio file with an app, it will save you time and energy to simply hire a freelancer or company to do this for you. It is best suited for those who do not want to put too much time and effort into editing their podcast. A freelancer or company will usually give you a better-quality audio file in much less time. Furthermore, you can save some extra time by hiring a team that already has all the necessary tools and equipment.

How Much Will It Cost?

Freelancers and companies will usually charge you anywhere from $10 to $20 for every fifteen minutes of audio they edit. This may vary depending on the company or freelancer, but this is a general standard rate. If your podcast is longer than an hour and a half, you may want to consider hiring two or three different companies or freelancers for this task.

If you go with a freelancer, it is important to look at their portfolio before sending them your audio file. This way, you will see the quality of their work. If you go with a company instead, check their references to see if they have worked on projects similar to yours in the past.

Why Should I Hire a Company to Edit My Podcast?

A company or agency whose business it is to edit podcasts will usually give you a better-quality audio file in much less time. They can usually produce your podcast within a few days, while freelancers may take several weeks to complete the job. It also saves you time and energy because the company or agency has experienced staff in editing podcasts.

Pros of Hiring a Company

Hiring a company to edit your podcast file is advantageous because they have the equipment, experience, and time to do it. They will give you the highest quality audio file in less time than freelancers can. You will not need to spend money on the necessary equipment or wait too long for your final copy.

Cons of Hiring a Company

Although you can expect a high-quality audio file from hiring a company or agency to edit your podcast, they will usually be more expensive than freelancers. You also will not have as much control over the final copy as you would with a freelancer. Moreover, if you want to adjust any of the editing done by the company, it will take longer for them to make the necessary changes.

Pros of Hiring a Freelancer

When you hire a freelancer to edit your podcast, you have more control over the final copy. Usually, they will send you a raw audio file or let you approve their changes before they post it online for listeners. It is also an affordable option compared with companies and agencies because it usually costs less than $20 per hour.

Cons of Hiring a Freelancer

You may have to wait a while with a freelancer before getting your final copy because one person usually processes it. Additionally, you probably will not receive a high-quality audio file from freelancers unless they have the necessary equipment and experience. It's also difficult to adjust the editing done by a freelancer because they may not make changes as quickly as you would like.

Things to Consider

Before you decide how to edit your podcast, you should decide if it will be one long file or include multiple episodes. If it is just one long file, companies and freelancers are better options than an app because of the editing done before the post-processing phase. If there are several episodes, you can look into apps that allow for this type of podcasting. While you do not need to know how to do the editing and post-production yourself, it's good to be aware of other options. You can decide what option is best for your podcast by considering costs, who will be doing the work, how long it will take them, delivery method (raw audio file or final copy), and the quality of the finished product.

If you decide on companies and agencies, be sure to look at the quality of their finished projects and their prices. If you go with freelancers, look at their resume and portfolio first before determining if they are the right fit for your podcast. Also, make sure that they have the necessary equipment or software to edit your podcast properly.

Podcasts continue to grow in popularity every day. Some businesses have even started using them as their primary marketing strategy compared to all of their other forms of advertising. Your podcast must be edited and post-produced to sound professional and reach your audience. Whether you want to edit and post-produce it yourself, hire a company, or use an app agency depends on what type of podcast it'll be and if multiple episodes will be included in the final file.

If you need to edit and post-produce your podcast, you should hire a company or agency first. You will get the highest quality file in the quickest amount of time for the best price. If multiple episodes are included in your final file, an app may be better for you because it's usually free and can prepare an edited audio file quickly without much hassle. If you want to do the editing and post-production yourself, it'll be the least expensive option but will take longer for your file to be complete.

Chapter 7: The Writing Stuff: Show Notes and Transcripts

Podcast show notes and transcripts are two really important but often overlooked pieces of the podcast puzzle. They are vital for SEO, easy reading, and accessibility purposes and can be a great takeaway for your listeners to use. There is no one way to write these and no real requirements other than to make them accessible for your listeners. This chapter will give you some tips for writing show notes and transcripts.

What Are Show Notes?

Show notes are what you use to post a list of your podcast episodes on your website, and they are often used for publishing transcripts. They're usually in bullet point form, with the episode title listed first, followed by the main talking points or topics covered in that episode. You can link to any relevant blog posts or images mentioned in the episode as well. A few things to remember are that people should be able to locate your show notes on your website without too much trouble, and the bullet points should be more or less in chronological order. Many podcast beginners just copy and paste their intro and outro for the show notes, though you can write it however you like.

Why Are They Important?

Podcast show notes are important because when you list the episode title and include links to any relevant blog posts or images, you give search engines like Google a way to index your podcast easily. All of this makes it much easier for people searching in Google or other search engines to find and listen to your podcast episodes. It is also really great for accessibility reasons. More and more people listen to podcasts on their mobile devices or while driving, and it can be hard for some listeners to follow along if there is no transcript.

How to Write Show Notes

At the time of writing this, there is not a single standard way to write your podcast show notes. Some may include almost everything from the episode in bullet point form, including personal thoughts and feelings about certain topics. All you have to do is make sure that it makes sense for your listeners, so try to keep the list chronological. If you have a guest on your podcast, it may be a good idea to include your conversation with that guest as bullet points as well. Just remember to keep the list short and sweet. Here is a step-by-step guide to writing podcast show notes:

1. Write a brief intro and conclusion for your show notes, and underline or bold the episode title so it stands out.
2. If applicable, list every main topic discussed in the episode as a bulleted point with a link to relevant blog posts or images.
3. List any conclusion or follow-up points under a "Conclusion" heading.
4. Include your thoughts and feelings about the episode if you want to—although it is also totally fine to leave those out. Remember, the goal of show notes is to easily guide listeners to find information on what was covered in each episode.

The Writing Stuff: Transcription

Transcription is when you write out the entire conversation in a podcast episode. It can be incredibly useful for people who are deaf or hard of hearing, and many podcasters choose to do it so their listeners can follow along easier. There is no single way or standard for transcription, and it may not be necessary in some cases. However, if you can do it, your listeners will appreciate it immensely.

Transcripts: Do I Need Them?

A transcript of your podcast recording can be a really valuable resource for many different reasons, but they are not 100 percent necessary. Many listeners prefer to listen to podcasts since it is easier than reading text. Having transcripts can also be helpful if people are listening with someone who is having a hard time following along or want to re-listen to something they heard before. If you go on YouTube or another video streaming service, chances are there will be a transcript available for your video. Transcripts are important for accessibility reasons, especially for the deaf or hard of hearing. It's also great for people who have slower Internet speeds and cannot stream the audio file to listen to your podcast. By listening to a transcription of the episode, they can get much more out of what was said.

Why Do I Need to Write Them?

While transcripts are not 100 percent necessary, podcasting experts have found that having written show notes or transcripts can drive up your SEO rankings in Google, so it might be worth it for you to write them if possible.

What Should They Include?

As mentioned earlier, show notes should be easy for listeners to follow along with and locate on your website. Including links to blog posts or images can also help, as long as it is not overwhelming for them. Short phrases or sentences about the topics covered in each episode are all you need. It will not be verbatim, but instead just something to give listeners a sense of what they will hear if they listen to the episode. Make sure they are accessible on your website without too much trouble, either by posting them on a separate page or including them at the end of each blog post.

Transcripts might be more work for you to create, but people who prefer reading will appreciate it if you take the time to do one. If you decide to go through the trouble of writing a transcript, you can save it as an Adobe Acrobat or HTML file. When creating written transcripts, make sure you include all important information, like the names of the speakers, titles, and musicians used for background music during the podcast recording. Remember that podcast listeners want to know what they will hear before they listen!

How to Transcribe Audio

While there is no one way to transcribe your audio file, here are some tools that may help:

1. *Express Scribe*: This is a versatile tool that you can download and add to your Chrome browser. It is easy to use, and most computers come with the Express Scribe software so you can record your voice.
2. *Microsoft Word or Google Docs*: Most writers are already familiar with these two applications, so it will be easy for them to type up what was said in each episode using these tools.
3. *Google Speech API*: This service is especially useful for podcasters who want to transcribe their episodes quickly and easily, and it is free and open-source as well! Using this API, you can go ahead and upload your audio file to the cloud, which will then return a text file of what was spoken in that episode. It also returns the timestamps of each word, making it easier for you to pinpoint and edit out any background noise or unnecessary words that were spoken in between what was relevant.
4. *Fi3M Speecy*: This is another free tool that allows you to upload an audio file and create a transcript from it within minutes! All you have to do is paste the URL of the audio file and wait for it to be processed. Once it returns, you can download your transcript in various file types—DOCX, TXT, HTML, and PDF.
5. *Transcribe*: This one costs $15 per month or $120 if you pay annually, but it might be well worth it. This tool is great for beginners because you can use their built-in presets, so you do not have to set up your preferences. It is also easy to export, so it saves a lot of time, plus the transcription will be pretty clean and professional sounding!

How to Make a Transcript for Podcasts

Transcriptions are the most time-consuming part of starting a podcast, but if you want to make your podcast accessible for every audience out there, you will need to take the time to create written transcripts for each episode. Whether or not you choose to transcribe each episode is up to you, but here is what to do when creating written transcripts:

1. If possible, use the same file format for all transcripts. This way, you can easily transfer one transcript to another if you are working on more than one episode at a time. Plain text is most common, so that is the recommendation.
2. Include the speaker's name and any sound effects or music cues in your written transcripts. It makes it easier for listeners to follow along if they can see who said what. If you use any background music or sound effects, make sure to include them, too!
3. Highlight the most important key points of your podcast. Nobody wants to read a lengthy transcript, so highlight the most important phrases and sentences. The

things that stand out should be included in your transcript, while the filler words and phrases can be left out.

4. Always include timestamps with each word. This will make it much easier for you to find where certain sounds or background noise start and end to edit them out later on. The Google Speech API mentioned above returns the timestamps of each word, so you might want to check that out if you are not sure how to do this yourself.

5. Edit and proofread your transcript as many times as possible! Editing is probably the most time-consuming part of transcribing or creating written transcripts, but it is worth taking the time to make them look nice. Spelling errors, bad grammar, typos, and incomplete sentences can all take away from the overall look of your transcript.

Podcast Transcripts vs. Written Transcriptions

There is a big difference between written transcripts and podcast transcripts. A written transcript is like reading a book or an article. It is not exactly dialogue, but it still gives you the gist of what was said without hearing any background noise. On the other hand, podcast transcripts are formatted as if they were dialogue from a conversation. Each person speaks for a certain amount of time before switching to the next speaker, and there are pauses between each speaker.

FAQs about Transcriptions for Podcasts

Here are some frequently asked questions about podcast transcripts:

1. *How long do podcast transcripts usually take to make?*

It depends on how many episodes you are transcribing, but for most people, it takes about an hour per episode. First, you need to transcribe your audio or hire someone else to do it for you, and then you need time to edit and proofread the transcript before it is ready to publish.

2. *Do I need special software to create transcripts?*

No, you do not need any special software for creating written transcripts for podcasts or videos in general. If you are transcribing already recorded audio, you will need something like Google Speech API so that your written transcripts are timed correctly. There are also plenty of free transcript-writing programs, so you may want to try searching the Internet for software if you don't have anything on your computer already.

3. *Do I still need written transcripts even if my podcast is mostly music?*

Yes! Even if your podcast does not contain much dialogue, written transcripts are still useful for accessibility purposes. All podcasts should have written transcripts, even if they are full of background noise and music.

4. *Do I need to hire a professional transcriptionist?*

In most cases, no! Many podcasters can handle the task of transcribing their episodes at first, but you might want to consider hiring a professional transcriptionist in the long run. It may be a bit costly, but having professionals do your transcriptions will save you a ton of time and energy.

When thinking about your podcast transcripts, remember that they are not just written transcripts of what was said. The format needs to be similar to a conversation, and you should highlight the most important phrases or sentences while leaving out the filler words and phrases. It may take a bit longer than expected during transcription and editing, but it is worth taking the time to produce high-quality transcripts that will attract more listeners and increase your view count.

Chapter 8: Where and How to Upload Your Podcast

The easiest way to get your podcast out there is to upload it online. Although you might have a small following, uploading your podcast to the popular directories can boost your audience and increase your chances of being discovered. Today's most popular podcast hosting sites will not only help you upload effortlessly but also integrate various podcast-related solutions into their websites, from tracking show downloads and analytics to creating transcripts, embedded players, and video recasts.

How to Upload Your Podcast to Podcast Hosting Sites

Uploading your podcast to a podcast hosting site is relatively easy. The only thing you need to have in place is an RSS feed, which contains the details of each episode you publish on your website. These details include the episode title, description, date and time of publishing, and a link to the MP3 file. To simplify creating an RSS feed for your podcast hosting site, you can use one of many WordPress plugins available for this purpose.

Once you have created your RSS feed and connected it with your account on a podcast hosting site, you can use any of its built-in tools to upload new episodes or update existing ones. You just need to find the right tool on a podcast hosting site and follow the steps specific to that particular tool. Once your episode is listed in a directory, people who discover it will have an easy way to access it. They will just need to click the "Play" button on its embedded player.

A podcast hosting site can help you upload your podcast episodes, and it can also boost your audience and increase your chances of being discovered through multiple avenues. Most podcasting directories offer statistics tools to track downloads and analyze how different episodes perform. They will also automatically update the details of your podcast across all directories so that you do not have to update them manually.

Many of the most popular podcast hosting sites will help you create transcripts for your episodes and embed player widgets in your website or blog. Podcast hosting services are easy to use, and they are also affordable for small independent podcasters. Some even have tiered pricing systems based on the number of monthly downloads you expect your podcast to receive. You can also take advantage of their free or money-back guarantees if, for some reason, you don't like how they work.

Where to Upload Your Podcast

Although no one directory will list all podcasts from all around the world, there are a few directories that you should consider uploading your podcast to.

Podcast hosting services will help you upload your podcast to these directories and more with minimal effort. While most of them use the RSS feed from your website, some can even integrate with iTunes and Google Play. They will also monitor any changes in your RSS feed so that all directories are updated automatically.

You can also upload your podcast to social networks such as Facebook and Twitter with the help of free or paid apps. Although you may have a hard time getting people on these networks to notice your podcast, they can do so in an easier way if your feed is already listed in a directory.

When choosing podcast hosting services, you will find dozens of companies offering similar features. The most important factor to consider is how well these features work on your website and what kind of support they offer. Most podcasting directories allow you to start with their free plans before upgrading later.

Podcasting Directories

Podcasting directories are websites that list podcasts and help users discover them; unlike search engines, which index web pages for keywords, podcast directories like iTunes or Stitcher use their algorithms to list relevant podcasts based on user requests and the directory's quality standards. The most popular podcast hosting sites are iTunes, Spotify, Google Podcasts, and TuneIn. By uploading your podcast on these directories, you can boost its visibility and attract a larger following.

The following is a list of the most popular podcasting directories and how to upload your podcast file to them:

iTunes Podcasts

When you publish a new episode on iTunes, it automatically gets downloaded to all subscribers of that particular podcast feed. This ensures that everyone has access to the latest episode, making them eager to listen, share, and rate it. iTunes is the most popular podcast directory, with over 2.8 million podcasts and 18 billion all-time downloads. Plus, their iOS Podcasts app has an enormous user base of 500 million monthly active users! To upload your podcast on iTunes, you will need to create an Apple ID, which is free of charge. Once logged in, click on "Podcasts" in the navigation menu and select "New Podcast." Fill out all your podcast's details and simply upload your episode file, cover art, and edit the other information. The feed should include cover art, episode titles, descriptions, and links to the file. iTunes accepts .mp3 or .m4a audio files less than 200 megabytes in size. It also provides the necessary RSS feed for your podcast to syndicate your show across all its platforms.

Google Podcasts

Unlike iTunes, Google Podcasts is a directory of all sorts of podcasts from across the web and not just from individual podcast hosts. The best part is that this also means that your show will be listed in Google Search along with other popular and trending shows. Because of this, make sure to make your podcast title catchy and "click-worthy" to get discovered!

Uploading your podcast to Google Podcasts is quite straightforward. You will need a Google account, which you can create for free on the web. Once logged in, go to "My Podcasts," click on "+New Episode," and upload your episode file (.mp3 or .m4a format). Ensure that your episode file is free of errors, or else Google may not approve it.

Spotify Podcasts

Although Spotify does not have a podcast directory, you can upload your audio files to their platform for free. This will allow you to access their audience of over 170 million global users. Moreover, as long as they follow the RSS feed and have a Spotify account, they can listen to your podcast.

To upload your podcast to Spotify, you will need the help of a podcast hosting site. You can use Buzzsprout or Podomatic to have your RSS feed verified by Spotify and list your show in their directory through the latter's free plan. Then just share a link to a song on Spotify, and your followers will be able to listen to it.

You may also direct your listeners to Spotify using the episode notes of each episode, much like you would with any other podcast directory. However, keep in mind that Spotify users are usually more engaged when they play songs, so make sure that your episodes are catchy enough for them to click on.

Stitcher

Another popular podcast directory is Stitcher, which can also host your audio files. With this service, you will get access to their audience of over 2 million registered users and upload your MP3 file for free. As with Spotify, make sure to use a podcast hosting site like Buzzsprout or Podomatic for your RSS feed verification.

With Stitcher, your podcast will be listed in their directory once they have verified your RSS feed. You can also opt to purchase a "Featured" status on their directory, which will allow you to promote your show as they will help share the episodes on social media and other sites and promote them on their platform.

Google Play Music

Google also has its podcast directory with Google Play Music to find all sorts of podcasts. Similar to iTunes, Google Play Music is not only for individual podcast hosts but includes several other popular and trending podcasts. The platform has an enormous user base of over 40 million subscribers who can listen to your show by accessing your RSS feed.

To submit your podcast to Google Play Music, you will need help from an external site like Podigee, which can automatically verify and upload your RSS feed for free. They also have a "Premium" plan that allows you to customize certain aspects of your listing, delete episodes, or even add in new ones at the click of a button.

However, if you want to skip the extra costs and list your podcast on Google Play Music for free, you can get in touch with Podigee's customer support to verify and upload your RSS feed over email. Just make sure you have all the necessary information they may need to verify your show.

TuneIn

Another highly popular directory is TuneIn, which has over 60 million users worldwide. This platform lets users listen to podcasts by first finding them in their directory and then streaming or saving them via apps like Stitcher, Google Play Music, etc. This directory is very similar to Stitcher since you will also need another external site to verify your RSS feed, which they call "TuneIn Direct."

To submit your podcast to TuneIn, make sure you have an RSS feed URL. You can create one on Buzzsprout or Podomatic for free with their respective free plans. Once you have that, fill out the form and wait for TuneIn's customer support to verify your RSS feed. Once they do, you will be able to submit your show in their directory.

Podcast Hosting Services

While you can have your RSS feed verified on several podcast directories via two different processes, it may be more efficient to just upload your file to a single platform that will integrate your podcast with multiple platforms. It will also allow you to monetize your podcast, distribute it worldwide, and track show statistics.

Here are some podcast hosting services that will also help you upload your show to multiple directories:

Buzzsprout

This popular podcast hosting site lets you host your RSS feed for free. You can sign up with them or upgrade later on, depending on what works best for you. After verifying your file, the next step is submitting it to different directories.

They have a list of all the podcast directories you can submit your RSS feed to and how to go about it for each one. You will first need an RSS Feed URL, which is generated on Buzzsprout after you sign up and verify your account. Then you can submit the file directly via their website by uploading it as an attachment.

Buzzsprout is a platform that allows you to upload MP3 files to their service for free. This tool keeps everything organized by ensuring that your episode or file gets updated in all directories simultaneously. Aside from directory integration, they also provide several other features like web hosting, spam protection, and marketing tools.

PodBean

This site lets you upload an MP3 file to their service in just a few seconds. Once your podcast is uploaded, they will host it on their server for free with advanced RSS Feed management, which makes sure that all directories are updated at the same time.

PodBean offers more features than Buzzsprout, letting you customize your podcast's RSS feed to fit your needs with their paid plans. You can also use their advanced analytics to track things like email signups and episode downloads, along with the price of each plan, depending on what works best for you.

To submit your podcast to their directory, you need the RSS Feed URL. This is automatically generated on PodBean after your MP3 file is uploaded. You can select the directories you want to submit it to via their dashboard based on whether or not they are free or require a yearly subscription fee.

Simplecast

This is another podcast hosting service that lets you upload your MP3 file, create an RSS feed, and submit it to various directories. They have a free plan that offers several features like statistics tracking, episode uploading, embeddable players, and more. Simplecast also integrates with WordPress sites to manage the publishing schedule of your podcast series on WordPress. This platform has a web-based dashboard where you can add and edit episodes, add show notes and images, update your feed information when necessary, and monitor your podcast's stats.

To upload your MP3 file to their service, you need the RSS Feed URL. They will also generate an ID3 tag and images for free in the process. For directories like Spotify and Google Podcasts, where they need a specific HTML description, you can add it via your Simplecast dashboard based on how many words it contains and its formatting.

Castos

This hosting platform lets you upload and manage your RSS feed for free. This site provides the necessary tools to assist podcasters with creating, marketing, optimizing, distributing, and monetizing their content online through its service.

Castos also has an editing tool to edit show descriptions and images for each episode before submitting it. This platform uses a simple, easy-to-navigate interface where you can manage your podcast directly on their website.

To upload your show to Castos, just click "Upload a Podcast" and follow the instructions. They will automatically generate an ID3 tag and images for free when uploading an MP3 file. Then you will be asked to select the directories where you want to submit your RSS feed.

YouTube

Since YouTube is the second largest search engine, it makes them a great place to start to attract additional traffic. You can upload your podcast to their service by creating a YouTube channel for your brand. Once you have an account, you can create a new video for each episode with the title and content of its show notes. The description should contain the entire transcript and relevant images that will be helpful when someone is trying to listen on the go using their mobile device.

You can also upload a video recording of yourself introducing your podcast or just talk about it briefly while showing screenshots and images. Viewers can subscribe to your channel, so they get notified every time you publish a new episode, making sure that it gets plenty of views. Once your video is ready, click "Publish" and choose the option to add it as an attachment.

PodBean, Buzzsprout, and Simplecast are just some of the many podcast hosting services you can use to upload your show. It is up to you which platform works best for you depending on what features, analytics tools, benefits, or price plans they offer.

Some podcast directories may need certain requirements and a paid plan before you can upload your file. Make sure to check their submission guidelines before proceeding.

Do not forget that you can also create an RSS feed on any podcast hosting site for free or upgrade later on, depending on what works best for you. It's always good to have a backup option in case one of the sites does not work out, along with web hosting, spam protection, and marketing tools that you should also look into before deciding which platform to go with.

Chapter 9: Podcasting for Profit: 10 Ways to Monetize Your Podcast

If you are thinking about monetizing your podcast, this chapter is for you! It will discuss the different ways podcasts can generate revenue. Just like any other business, podcasts need to bring in income to survive. That is where advertising, sponsorships, subscriptions, referral programs, and affiliate marketing come into play. The following tips and strategies may not apply to every podcaster, but they should give you a good overview of what options exist to generate profit.

Remember that the most important thing is to give value. Your listeners need to know they can trust you and get something of value from listening, watching, or reading what you offer; otherwise, there will be no point in them continuing their association with you. If what you are producing is good, you should not have to worry about monetizing. People will want what you're selling.

Here are a few practical tips and strategies on monetizing your podcast:

   1. **Advertising (Online)**

This may be the simplest way for a beginner podcaster to bring in revenue, but this option will not be very relevant or effective if your podcast has a small audience and/or you are just starting out in podcasting.

There are different types of advertising that you can use to generate income for your podcast. You basically have two options: direct sponsorship or affiliate marketing.

Sponsorship works just like it sounds. Someone pays for your show directly to share their message with your audience (and vice versa). This is the more traditional form of advertising and tends to be used by larger podcasts.

It involves you advertising their product by using phrases such as, "This podcast is brought to you by…" or "I'm going to be talking about…" You need to get approval from the company before you can start advertising their product or service.

However, sponsors are not really going to be interested in your podcast if you do not have much traffic or listeners. You can always start with a list of people you are already in touch with and work from there. You can also target sponsors relevant to your show's topic(s) and have a smaller audience.

If you have a relatively smaller audience, *affiliate marketing* will probably be a better option. This essentially means that someone is willing to pay you in return for linking back and/or promoting their product or sometimes service.

This can be through affiliate marketing networks, such as Commission Junction, ShareASale, or Amazon.

Affiliate marketing involves you promoting a product or service and earning money for each sale that results from your podcast listeners clicking on your affiliate link, going to the merchant's site, and purchasing something. Then they will be redirected back to the vendor through your unique code. You will typically say, "Start investing in stocks easily, click here." or "Check out this online store and use the promo code 'XYZ' for a free gift."

Risks involved in Sponsorship and Affiliate Marketing

- To be really profitable, you need to have a large audience for this monetization strategy.
- The consumer may not feel they got the best deal from both parties because there is no actual sale taking place, but rather just two businesses coming together for their mutual benefit (rather than one party selling directly to another).
- The company may discontinue the affiliate product or service, leaving you in the lurch, especially if it is your sole source of income.

Sponsorship and affiliate marketing allow you to generate income for your podcast by selling advertising space. However, there are other ways that podcasters make money online outside of these traditional forms of monetizing their podcasts.

2. **Selling a Subscription to Your Listeners**

If you have a large audience for your podcast, selling a subscription is an option that can be effective. This involves offering exclusive content to subscribers in exchange for their email address and sometimes even credit card information. You could also offer additional perks, such as early access or discounts on merchandise.

Setting up membership tiers for your subscription service is a good idea to attract different audiences. You could have things like "Free Access," where the user will access special content but not pay anything for it. Then you can give them "Premium Access," which includes paying members getting early access and other perks before anyone else sees the content. Finally, you can also make your most premium subscription "VIP," which includes personalized customer service and other exclusive benefits!

This is not an option for podcasters who do not have a large audience yet because it requires more listeners to be successful (but if you are already getting lots of downloads/subscribers, it's definitely a good idea).

Another important aspect is to be wary of the fact that you might end up losing your audience if too much of your content is behind a paywall. This is why it's important to provide enough free content so that people are still willing to come back.

Use tools such as Patreon, PodBean, or Podia to monetize your podcast by offering subscriptions to your listeners.

3. Advertising Your Products and/or Service

Another method that podcasters can use to monetize their podcast is promoting their products or services. This could be through advertising on the actual podcast episode itself, in an email newsletter sent out before or after a new show goes live, in blog posts, or even in social media posts.

This type of monetization is typically easy to do because you are simply talking about your business and products during the podcast! You can be creative with this by adding something like, "If you're interested in buying the product I discuss on today's show, go to our website at..." and then provide a link to the product you're talking about.

For instance, if it's an ad for your book (and you're using these ads as promotional tools), mention that section of the book where this particular idea or information is found because people love diving into books and reading detailed descriptions!

If your podcast is about a particular product or service that you provide, constantly talk about it throughout the podcast. For example, if you run a plumbing company and your podcast is about home maintenance tips, frequently talk about the services you provide for people with clogged drains.

Product/Service Ideas You Can Provide

eBooks and Reports

eBooks and reports can be very useful for people looking to learn more about your topic. Plus, you could include affiliate links within the actual book/report itself, but it would be helpful to mention that information during the podcast so people know this!

You could also include these books/reports in your membership subscription service for additional perks. For instance, if someone pays $25 per month to be a member of your "Plumbing Club," and the book you mention is only available as part of their subscription (and not on its own), they may opt for it.

Another great idea is to offer some of your books/reports for free or at a discounted rate if someone opts in for an email newsletter that you have! This can be another promotional tool to get more people interested in what you are doing and build trust with your audience.

Webinars

Webinars are a great way to educate people on your topic. You can then sell products and services you have during the webinar by providing information about what they might need if they want specific solutions or answers for their problems.

Online Courses

You could create online courses by recording videos of yourself teaching something related to your topic and then sell these courses via affiliate links, membership subscriptions, or through an eCommerce store.

Use platforms like Udemy or Teachable to sell your courses.

Speeches, Seminars, and Workshops

If you are good at public speaking or have knowledge in a certain area that would be beneficial for others to learn about, this could also be an option! You can talk more about how to get started with creating speeches/seminars/workshops and how to make money with them. You can do this by charging admission for your event and creating a website where people can learn more about what they would get if they become members or sign up.

4. **Personal Consultation**

You can offer personal consulting sessions where you are paid to help people with whatever they need. You could charge per hour or for a certain number of hours (for example, $100/hour). These services are typically provided via Skype, and you will likely be working directly with one person at a time.

You could also offer some of these services for free (for example, if someone subscribes to your email newsletter) and then charge a fee when you have finished helping them solve whatever issue they may have had. This is where that "honesty factor" comes into play because it keeps people coming back!

5. **Sell Branded Merchandise**

You could sell branded merchandise on your website or platforms like Etsy. For example, if you have a dog training podcast and decide to create T-shirts with funny phrases about dogs being "potty trained," all of the profits will go directly into your pocket! You can also include affiliate links within these shops so you can still make some money when someone buys something.

Another interesting thing is to create a poll and ask your podcast audience members what they would like to see (shirt colors, designs, etc.), and then send them links that go directly to where they can purchase the items.

6. Charge for Older Podcast Episodes

You could charge for access to older podcast episodes since it is likely that you have a lot of past content and information available on your website. This is another good reason why having an email newsletter list is important because then people will need to subscribe for this option to work (plus, they can unsubscribe whenever they like).

7. Offering Sponsorships

If you have a podcast with at least 100–500 listeners per episode, advertisers are likely to be interested in sponsoring your show. You can do so by being active on iTunes and submitting your podcast for approval (you will need an Apple ID). After this has been approved, go into the "settings" section of your podcast and click on "sponsorship." You can choose how many episodes per month you would like to offer and what price they will be (you could also make these customizable).

The more active iTunes is for your podcast, the better chances advertisers have at seeing it and contacting you to see if you are interested in a sponsorship opportunity.

This is how to monetize your podcast! There are other options available not mentioned here, but these are the most tried and tested ideas and should give you a good idea of what works and the best ways to get started making money with your podcast today. It is important to note that this strategy does not work if your podcast is not getting a decent number of downloads per episode. You'll need to get more listeners for this model to work, but it's possible if you're passionate about what you do and willing to put in the effort!

8. Publishing Podcasts on YouTube

Another thing you could do is publish your episodes on YouTube. This will mean that the videos are available to watch at any time, and they will not get deleted after a certain amount of time, so people can binge-watch them whenever they like! You may even choose to film yourself reading the podcast's content and then upload it as a video to your channel. Either way, this is another great option that can help you reach more people who may not have otherwise known about your show!

9. Listener Donations

You could always just ask for donations. All you need to do is let people know how they can donate, offer additional resources if someone decides to donate (more valuable content, access to private discussions on Facebook groups, etc.), and then reach out personally when they are available to set up their payment.

This is a great option if you do not have the resources to set up advertisements or sponsorships on your podcast. This will work best if you already have an audience built and ready, but it is also possible to reach out to people who may be interested in donating once they have listened to at least one episode. Just make sure that you are offering something in return for their money.

10. Invite and Interview Guests

You could invite other people to be interviewed on your podcast or have them share their expertise within an episode. This is another great way to get more listeners because they will hear you speaking with experts in the field, and it will make you look like a credible source of information!

You can choose how many episodes per month you would like to offer and what price they will be; you could also make these customizable.

It is important to note that this strategy may not fit all podcasts. For example, if you have a podcast about personal finance, interviewing people who are also great sources of knowledge on this topic might make sense, but if your podcast is about stories or your personal life, this might not be as appropriate.

How Much Money Can Be Made with a Podcast?

Each monetization technique will give you different returns. The beauty is in volume. If you have a couple of hundred listeners per episode, you may not make much. If you have thousands of listeners per episode, the sky is the limit.

As per statistics from the average CPM, the cost per 1,000 listeners is $18 for thirty seconds and $25 for sixty seconds.

Noteworthy podcasts such as The American Life, with approximately 800,000 downloads per episode, earn about $40 for every 1,000 listens, which means an average of $32,000 per episode! Now that is the benchmark. Tim Ferris's "The Tim Ferriss Show" podcast reportedly makes about $100,000 per episode!

How much time does it take to start making real money on your podcast?

As for how long it takes before the money starts rolling in, that depends on your podcast and audience size. The more popular your show becomes, the faster this will happen! Typically, the time it takes to start making money with your podcast is between six months and a year.

Obviously, it is not an overnight success story across the board, but seeing how you progress over time can be really fun. So yes, "it depends," but it's not something that takes forever to get started with, and there is potential for some income along the way.

What are the most common mistakes to avoid when monetizing a podcast?

One of the biggest mistakes podcasters make is not having enough episodes. A great way to increase your audience size is by uploading new episodes frequently (once or twice per week). If you upload only once every month, this will be very difficult for people to follow.

Another mistake people make is not spending enough time on a decent-looking website or blog to post their content. You want to have great-looking artwork as well as an email signup form on your site so you can build up your mailing list and continue connecting with listeners after the episode has ended!

Focus on quality and creating a great experience for your listeners, and you will be in an excellent position to monetize. If people feel like they are investing time in the content, there is much more of a chance that they will return and keep listening!

Advertise your podcast to build a loyal audience first and then focus on monetizing your show.

Where to Begin?

If you would like to start monetizing your podcast, the first thing to do is look at iTunes and find some podcasts that are similar in style to what you would like to do.

What do they talk about? How often do they release new episodes (weekly, monthly)? What kind of artwork or logo does their show have? How might this help or hinder them from being discovered by listeners?

Once you have a clear idea of what makes a successful podcast, start building your brand.

As with any online business, the most important thing is to think about how you can help people and where they may be looking for that kind of information. Once you know that, it is much easier to create something that will answer their questions and stand out from the competition.

The next step is to start connecting with other podcasters and influencers in your niche, share their content, interact on social media — generally, be helpful where you can. This will help to position yourself as an expert early on, which makes it much easier for people to trust your recommendations down the line when you have a monetization strategy in place.

This works even better if you can get a guest spot on another show, but make sure you give them something valuable before asking for anything back. This could be your podcast episode or a blog post they may share with their audience.

And finally—just start creating content and building a mailing list from day one! You can offer some kind of freebie that your listeners can only access by providing you with certain contact information. This is the most effective way to get started with podcasting and eventually make money on it, too!

There are many ways to monetize your podcast. Whether you are just getting started or have been producing podcasts for a while, now is the time to start thinking about how to make money from your show. The key is to connect with people and provide value to build trust before asking them for anything in return! It's also important to think about how much work goes into creating content and what kind of experience you want listeners to come back for? If they feel like they are investing their time listening each week, there is likely more interest on their end when considering monetization strategies.

Chapter 10: Marketing Your Podcast

As a relatively new form of media, podcasts have taken the Internet by storm—and the fact that anyone who has an idea can create a podcast and share it is unprecedented. However, not everyone knows how to market their podcast effectively, which separates the truly creative from the hobbyists regarding audiences or listeners. This chapter will cover marketing your podcast on social media, consistency in content production, building an audience through hosting giveaways, and other forms of advertising and promotion.

Using Social Media for Podcast Marketing

When it comes to marketing and promoting your podcast, social media is an excellent place to start. Since there are many options available, this chapter will cover the most popular ones that people use to promote their podcasts.

Twitter

Twitter allows you to upload 140 character long posts called tweets, which may contain links to other websites. When you create an account for your podcast, use the same name that you have used on iTunes and your homepage because this will help people find your podcast easier when looking through their feed or searching specific hashtags like #podcasts.

Tips for Marketing on Twitter

The best time to tweet about your podcast is during the peak activity hours of the day, which for Twitter is usually between noon and midnight. Tweeting during this time will help you get more eyes on your post. However, do not try to promote at odd hours because users will not see your tweet.

Post often and keep your content confined to news about your podcast, blog, or episode so you can gain more potential followers. However, do not overdo it by tweeting too much because Twitter is a place for brief posts, and people may unfollow you if they feel you are spamming their feed.

Engage with your followers by replying to their tweets and asking them questions. This will help build a community around the podcast, so people feel more inclined to listen, which leads to your audience downloading episodes and sharing with other people.

Instagram

Instagram is an online platform where users post pictures, videos, and stories. The idea behind the site is to create a community of people who share the same interests and interact with one another. Instagram can be used in several ways when it comes to podcast marketing. It is important to create a brand identity for your podcast by having a cohesive look running through your brand, which means you should have a specific background color and logo. People will remember the aesthetics of your account, so it is important to have an individual and engaging look.

In addition, it's important to use hashtags when you post so people can find your account and your posts. The best way to choose hashtags is by using ones that are specifically about your podcast or its topic, for example, #podcasts or #podcasting.

Hashtags are effective because they are simple for people to navigate, and they can find other accounts that share similar interests, which helps to grow your brand.

Use reels to promote your podcast. They are quick videos you can make using Instagram's new feature. People tend to watch reels in full, so this can be a great way to get people to listen and engage.

Be sure to respond to everyone who comments on your posts. This is an excellent way for you and the person to connect, which could lead them to listen to your podcast!

IGTV is a new feature for Instagram where people can post long videos (similar to YouTube). This platform allows you—the user—to upload your video directly on Instagram instead of linking it to another site. This is beneficial because you can watch the video directly through your feed without having to navigate to a separate site—Instagram likes that.

Tips for Marketing on Instagram

People tend to post on Instagram more during the mornings and afternoons, so it is a good idea to promote your account during these times.

Use your bio to promote your podcast or blog post. You can also include a link and an email address so people know where you are based and how they can contact you.

Post often and engage with your community whenever possible because this will help build a sense of trust between the people following your account.

Post useful content that will engage your followers. People typically follow accounts that they find interesting, so it is important to keep them interested!

Use tools like IFTTT, Buffer, and Hootsuite to schedule your posts so you can have a steady flow of information about your podcast.

Consider posting just before you release a podcast episode so people can get excited and listen to your new episode.

Tiktok

Tiktok is a popular social media platform that can be used similarly to Instagram. However, this site is specifically used to create videos. This is the same idea behind Instagram's reels.

Tips for Marketing on Tiktok

As with all social media platforms, it is important to create a cohesive brand identity for easy recognition concerning the aesthetics of your account.

You can use hashtags when you post for people to find your posts and follow you.

Use videos to promote your podcast. People tend to watch these longer than pictures or reels, so this is a good way for you to get people interested in your podcast and grow your audience.

Show off what you are doing and how it relates to the topic of your podcast so that people can become engaged with your account.

As with Instagram, post often, especially if you are promoting an event or a new podcast episode. This will help build interest in your account and your podcast.

Facebook Pages and Groups

On Facebook, people have the option to create pages or groups. These can be used as a way for you to interact with your audience and promote your podcast.

Tips for Marketing on Facebook

Use your page or group to promote new episodes of your podcast and host giveaways that can be shared on your page.

People can like pages and groups on Facebook, which means it is important to make an engaging post that will get people excited about your podcast.

Facebook live allows you to broadcast live videos on your page so people can see what you are doing and engage with it in real-time.

There are also ways to market your podcast on Facebook with ads. These can be used as a way for people to discover and listen to your podcast.

Influencer Marketing

When you start out with your podcast, it is important to begin building up your social media presence. One effective way of doing this is by partnering up with influencers. Influencer marketing is a great way to increase brand awareness and give your podcast the boost it needs in the early stages. Influencers are people who have a high following on social media and will help your podcast get noticed.

Some influencer marketing techniques you could consider are interviewing an influencer on your podcast or even collaborating with them to create a content piece jointly.

Interviewing an influencer gives people who already know and trust their opinion another reason to subscribe. If they have never heard of your show before, this is where they may find out about what you do.

Collaborating with influencers will help increase brand awareness and cross-promoting each other's shows.

Do not be afraid to ask for collaborations if the opportunity presents itself because, often, these requests can lead to big opportunities. You just need to play it by ear and see how things go when you reach out!

Market Your Podcast on Your Blog

If you have a blog, one way to promote your podcast is by creating a "show notes" post where you link back to each podcast episode and include a summary of what was discussed. You can also link back to each episode in the posts on your blog so people know where to listen.

Tips for Marketing on Your Blog

People can subscribe through email or RSS feeds, which will help increase the number of people who listen to your podcast and increase the likelihood of people finding you.

Create a custom landing page for your podcast and share links for listening options to other platforms, such as Spotify, iTunes, or direct download links.

You may even write blog posts that complement each episode of your podcast. In them, you can write a summary of what was discussed and post links to any relevant resources mentioned on the podcast.

This can be useful for attracting new listeners and creating engagement with your existing audience, as well as increasing the popularity of your blog.

Guest Post on Other Blogs

If you are an expert on your podcast topic, consider guest posting for others. This is a great way to promote yourself and your podcast.

Guest posts are a great way to build up an audience of people who may not find your podcast, and you can draw a larger audience to your site, blog, and social media accounts.

Leaving a link at the end of your guest post will help people discover your podcast and listen to the available episodes.

Guest posting is also a great way to build up credibility with others in your industry. People will see that you are knowledgeable and an authority on the topic of your podcast, which will help them trust and respect you.

Using Quora, Yahoo! Answers, LinkedIn

Other promotional platforms are sites like Quora. People can ask questions about your topic, and you can answer them as well as promote your podcast.

This is a great way for people to discover your account and listen to your podcast. Include links back to each podcast episode so people can listen and subscribe easily. The idea is to use as many platforms as possible, but remember to target your audience correctly and be discerning about your choice of platform, depending on the type of people you are targeting.

Medium

Medium is another great platform for you to share your podcast with others. By publishing articles on Medium, you get exposure to a whole different audience. Medium also allows other users to republish your content so that it gets even wider exposure! This is a huge opportunity because the more times someone sees or hears about your podcast, the better chance they will subscribe to it.

Podcast Directories

Using appropriate directories can help increase your discoverability. Podcast directories are beneficial when used correctly because they allow listeners access to new podcasts along with yours through search functionality. It is easy for listeners who do not know what shows are available or where else they can search to find your podcast.

You can also add the "Podcast" tags when you publish a blog post or an article about your show so that people who are searching for podcasts related to yours, in particular, can find and listen to it.

Paid Promotions

If you have a budget to promote your podcast, consider using paid advertisements. Paid promotions can be used as a way for people to discover and listen to your podcast, as well as increase the popularity of your blog.

Platforms such as Facebook and Instagram are great for paid promotions. These platforms allow you to target specific users interested in your podcast and help track the effectiveness of your ads.

Consider running a small ad campaign to test the effectiveness and viability of paid promotions for your podcast, as well as attract new listeners.

You can even get established podcasts to mention your show to help increase awareness of your podcast. This can be done by emailing and asking if they would be willing to promote your podcast. Some podcasts are even listed on online portals that ask for a fixed price to feature their advertisement in your show.

If you have been featured on another podcast, always mention them in yours, as it builds goodwill and is a great cross-marketing ploy.

Advertising in Podcast Apps

If you have a budget for promotions, another idea is to use it through advertising in podcast apps. Apps such as Overcast(iOS) allow you to purchase ad space inside their app. This can be an effective way to increase the number of new listeners and grow your following.

It is crucial to select the right category to advertise to reach the right audience. Ads should be placed in a category related to your podcast while being relatively close to the top of the list so that new listeners can easily discover them.

Podcast Addict is another such app that allows you to advertise your show. You can choose between categories related to the topic of your podcast, which is a great way for people interested in your topic to discover your show.

With the right promotions, you can see an increase in listenership and subscribers!

Offer Free Downloads

A great way to increase awareness of your podcast is to offer free downloads for any episode that you publish.

Offering free downloads can help people discover your podcast and increase the number of subscribers. Offering a way for listeners to download your episode for free will encourage them to subscribe and listen regularly.

The freebie could be anything related to the podcast, such as a summary of important points made in an episode or even just the audio file itself. If you host a finance podcast, it could be a downloadable excel sheet calculator. If your podcast is about music, you could offer free guitar lessons.

This is a great way to encourage new listeners!

Encourage Sharing

Another way to promote your podcast and attract new listeners is by encouraging people to share episodes. This can be done using social media platforms, like Facebook or Twitter. People will naturally want to share the episode with their friends if they enjoy it, which helps increase awareness of your show while growing your following. You can also encourage sharing on other websites, like Reddit.

Encouraging sharing helps people discover your podcast through word of mouth, which is one of the best ways to gain new listeners.

Host Giveaways

Hosting giveaways is a great way to continue growing your podcast and expand the number of subscribers you have. Host giveaways for any occasion—a national holiday, or even just to celebrate the New Year. Giveaways are a great way for people who do not know about your podcast to discover your show.

The prize for the giveaway could be anything that relates to your podcast. It can even be an item with your logo to help increase awareness of who you are and what your podcast is about.

If you want to get extra creative, consider creating a custom T-shirt with your podcast logo on it and use them as prizes and giveaways. This can help increase awareness of your podcast while also being a fun way to get new listeners.

Giveaways can be hosted on your blog, Instagram, YouTube Live Session, or Facebook page. If you can bring in a unique gift to giveaway, it creates a buzz around your show and helps attract new listeners.

Some great giveaway ideas are books related to the topic of your podcast or even a gift card. The more creative you can get with these gifts, the better!

The Importance of Consistency

Many people will initially subscribe to your podcast but then forget about it or lose interest. To avoid this loss of listenership, consider how often you publish.

People like to know when they can expect your next episode to be published, and a regular schedule will help you avoid losing listeners. If you cannot publish regularly, consider publishing once every two weeks or even every month!

It is also important to remain consistent across your social media platforms. When you post new content across your social media platforms, make sure that it is on a regular schedule so people know when they can expect new content.

Posting on a regular schedule will help with brand awareness and encourage people to subscribe.

Today, with the amount of content online, out of sight means out of mind. That is why it is vital to remain fresh and consistent across all your platforms. Do not let your audience forget you.

Another important trick could be to release a periodic newsletter. This is a great way for people to know when new content has been added and will help you gain extra subscribers. The more you keep your audience in the loop, the better!

When to Start Marketing Your Podcast?

It is important to begin marketing your podcast as soon as you have created the first episode. If you are just starting out, it is important to get the word out.

The more you can create buzz about your podcast before it actually releases, the better. You can do this by creating a teaser video or trailer for your show and putting it up across the different social media platforms you have planned to use in your marketing strategy.

When you set your show to "live" on your social media platforms, make sure you engage with the audience and encourage them to subscribe. You can also ask for feedback and suggestions about your show.

Having an engaging show will help people keep coming back for more.

The first step in marketing your podcast is understanding whom you are trying to target and what best appeals to them regarding language and aesthetics.

Choose your audience carefully and do not try for a broad market straight away; be strategic in your marketing plan. Focus on attracting a specific niche audience interested in the podcast's topic.

Once you have defined your target audience, it will be easier to start marketing. You can promote your podcast through social media posts and by engaging with online communities and groups that your target audience is a part of.

If you want to get more creative, consider hosting giveaways on social media or your podcast. Hosting giveaways is a great way to attract new listeners and grow your show.

It is also important to be consistent with your podcast publishing schedule and publishing across your social media platforms. If people know when to expect new podcasts and videos from you, it will be easier to attract an audience.

Chapter 11: Guest Interviewing Skills

The previous chapters mentioned everything you need to know about starting a podcast. From finding the right topics and targeting your audience to all the technicalities and how to make money from your show, you should now have a good idea of how to launch your podcast. Now it is time to learn about some essential skills you will need when interviewing your guests on the show. Guests can be one of the main contributors to the success and continuity of your podcast. This chapter details what kind of guests to bring to your show, how to improve your guest interviewing skills, and how to present an interesting topic to discuss on your podcast.

How to Find the Perfect Guests for Your Show

One of the biggest challenges when running your podcast is searching for the best guests for your show. You need to learn how to approach the right people to appear on your show. First of all, find out what other shows cover similar topics as yours. Make a list of the guests who have appeared on them and do some research to determine if they are the right fit for your podcast. Most people who appeared on previous shows will probably want to do it again. If you can get them on your show, you have to make sure that you provide a different perspective. Make sure while you are planning that you do not repeat any content that may have been heard on someone else's show. You want your interview to stand out from others to provide a fresh, interesting show for your guest and audience. Another great tip for finding guests is to search for other bloggers or YouTubers who tackle the same issues as your show does. By convincing them to appear as guests on your podcast, you will benefit from their followers tuning in on your show, which gives you better exposure. This collaboration will also benefit the audience because you'll present them with relatable content. Other potential guests can be people who appear on television or radio channels or write in magazines and newspapers. People working on different media platforms love to be given the chance to expand their audience, and your podcast would be the perfect place to do that.

One of the best ways to find guests for your show is to search for authors who wrote about a topic related to your content. Writers usually jump at the chance to be guests on shows to promote their books. They will benefit from your audience, and you'll benefit from having a professional talking about your selected topic. Bear in mind that this interview is not about encouraging people to buy the book but to start a healthy conversation. You must aim for a show with valuable insights for your audience because they always have to be your main target. Attracting audiences means higher ratings for your show, ensuring its continuity and success. The audience can easily spot a fake interview meant as a sales pitch for the book, so be careful when planning a show with a published author.

It is vital to sit with your guest before the show and go through some of the main points you will cover so that both of you are on track with the flow of the interview. Explain to them that they will still be able to talk about their book at the end of the interview — to give them a chance to promote it without it being the main theme of the interview. As you are ending the show, you can mention to the audience where they can get the author's book. Your main goal is to talk about the subject at hand, and then you can briefly mention how the book contains further details and insights about the topic.

You can also ask your current guests about potential people who might want to come in for an interview on your podcast. Just ask them right after your interview with them, or you can follow up with them in an email to ask for recommendations. This will help convince other potential collaborators to appear on your show since they were referred to by someone they already know, which increases your chances of getting another guest on a future episode. If you had a successful interview with your guest, chances are they'll be willing to refer you to other people.

Do not forget to engage your audience in your decisions. Many podcast and radio hosts will ask their audience for suggestions of experts or celebrities they would like to hear. Making your audience feel that they are part of the decision-making process is an excellent idea to get them interested and hooked, especially when you can get the people they suggested as guests. Make it a habit to tell people to share their opinions on your page at the end of every episode, and don't forget to reply to all of their messages, as being active matters to your audience. You can also create a simple form for people interested in appearing on your show so that you can get a good idea of who would be a good fit for the next episode.

To approach potential guests, it is best to send them a formal email inviting them to talk on your show. Give a brief outline of what your show is about and the main points you would like to tackle in the upcoming episode. Avoid being too formal, as you want to get the person excited. Limiting your email to three paragraphs is also important, as most people will be put off by a long email. Remember, it's an invitation, not an article. You just need to introduce yourself and your show, mention the subject that will be discussed, and tell them how you think their appearance would benefit them and the audience. You can also add how you know about them or if another guest referred them to you so that they'll be more interested in joining your show.

If you approach a celebrity, you have to be smart about it. An email might not suffice in this case, as yours would probably end up in the junk folder or drown in a sea of emails that they probably get every day. Instead, you may want to record a voice message or a short video about why you think this collaboration would be a great fit. You can use social media platforms, in this case, by tagging a certain celebrity to a video posted in your account. Of course, you have to make sure that the celebrity is active on these platforms and whether or not they respond to such messages.

The above tips are just a few ways to approach guests for your podcast. Remember that your focus should be on your topic and audience before even thinking about a guest. Try to mix it up by having a guest co-host the show with you on that episode. Interacting with your audience is an important indicator of which guests to invite back to your show; you can even have a regular guest come in one day a week if people ask for them. You can conduct regular polls on your page to determine what your audience thinks about your guests.

How to Improve Your Guest Interviewing Skills

It is time to discuss the dynamic between you — as the host — and your guest and how the interview should be conducted. The first thing you need to do is prepare by doing thorough research. You need to know everything about the topic to be discussed and the full bio of your guest. Prepare an outline of the show, starting from your introduction of your guest to the questions you will ask them throughout the episode. Rehearse your script at home several times to prepare yourself mentally for the interview. Get plenty of rest the day before the interview, and make sure you arrive early to get yourself comfortable. When your guest sees that you are well prepared, it will help them feel at ease to allow you to take the lead.

Just as you prepare yourself for the interview, you must prepare your guest. You need to tell your guest whether your podcast will be audio recorded only or if it's going to be shot on camera as well. Take ten to fifteen minutes before the show to brief your guest on how the episode will advance. Make sure they know what the topic is and how you'll discuss each question.

It's important to be an active listener to your guest. Do not interrupt them to make a point, but rather give them the space to voice their opinion before moving on to another point. Ask your questions clearly, and then wait for them to respond. You can only intervene if you feel they have trouble concentrating or getting an idea through, so you need to be mindful of their facial expressions and body language to know when to cut in. Be as honest as possible with your guest and allow them to be themselves. It's important that your guest feels at ease as they speak, which is how they connect to the audience. Your research about the guest will tell you some details that you might introduce to them to make them laugh or get them surprised that you know such information. This might be a hobby they had as a child or a funny anecdote that you got from a family member. These details are what will make your guest feel you cared enough to find out about them, which is an excellent ice breaker and a great way to get them speaking freely. Having a few laughs with your guest will get the listeners invested and interested in what you have to say because it seems you're having fun doing it! In the end, remember to give a shout-out to your guest's book, product, or social media accounts, as it's a great way to acknowledge their work.

How to Present an Interesting Topic on Your Show

When planning a show, you have to find a topic that appeals to your audience. You need to learn how to start a healthy conversation about your topic. Although it is important to keep things friendly on a podcast, it's also better to dig deeper into a subject. Ask your guest about their history and how they were able to get to where they are. Emphasize their journey and how they overcame any obstacles they faced. Personal struggles are relatable, and the audience appreciates learning about people's success stories.

Be mindful of hints your guest gives while telling their story. You can ask them further questions about their life, which can turn out to be a good surprise for the audience. Remember that it's okay to be flexible and change the pace of the episode a bit, and not everything has to go exactly as planned. Talk to your audience in between your conversation and ask them to share their opinions on your page, or you can have them ask questions to your guest that you can discuss on air.

Ask your guest about the things they wish they knew before starting their career. This gets the audience interested in hearing their story, especially if they are about to enter the same field. Let your guest talk about their mistakes and how they learned from them, and if they have any advice to give to the audience. It's also a good tip to let the listeners know about any resources the guest used in their career. In the end, ask the guest about how the listeners can contact them, which also gives the guest the chance to promote their pages.

As the host, you must know when to pause and let your guest speak and when to ask your question and intervene. You want to keep the episode flowing smoothly, so a change of pace is needed, especially if you are conducting a long interview. Listen to your favorite podcasts and learn how the hosts keep the conversation flowing, and keep notes that you can use with your next guest.

Conclusion

Starting a podcast does not feel so daunting anymore, does it?

As you saw with this informative guide to starting a podcast, the process is pretty simple. The areas that often stump people are equipment, editing, and uploading. However, this book covered all three of them in detail.

Thus, there you have it: the steps to starting a podcast. These are just general guidelines that can help you get started on your podcasting journey. There is so much more information and technicalities involved in getting your show off the ground and keeping it up and running, so use this book as your starting block as it is a solid foundation to build on as you embark on your podcasting journey.

Good luck!